Mobile Genealogy:

How to Use Your Tablet and Smartphone for Family History Research

iOS & Android

Lisa Louise Cooke

Contributors

Lacey Cooke, Vienna Thomas

Disclaimer:

The tablet apps and features, and related websites discussed in this book are constantly evolving. It's only natural that some of the websites and tools I refer to and points I mention in this book will change over time, which is out of my control. The good news is that you can tune in to the Genealogy Gems Podcast at www.GenealogyGems.com and other online resources to get the latest updates.

Also keep in mind that in this book we are not just covering step-by-step instructions but also overarching concepts. These concepts will serve you well even if websites or other data change. And of course, you can always tap into the Help section of any app or website for specific problem solving information.

Additional items by Lisa Louise Cooke available at www.genealogygems.com:

Books:

Genealogy Gems: Ultimate Research Strategies, 2007

Turn Your iPad into a Genealogy Powerhouse, 2012

How to Find Your Family History in Newspapers, 2012

The Genealogist's Google Toolbox 2nd Edition, 2015

CDs:

Google Earth for Genealogy Volume I

Google Earth for Genealogy Volume II

Acknowledgment

Keeping up with technology is more than a full-time job for me. Even then, a book like this could not be possible without the help of others.

I want to thank two talented women who I admire and trust. The first is my daughter Vienna Thomas. She has an eagle eye for grammar and punctuation. She also had endless patience for my editing and research requests, and that is saying something because she is a full-time mom to two energetic sons.

The second is my daughter Lacey Cooke. While Lacey has assisted with previous books, she stepped up in a big way on this one. Her editing was invaluable because she operated as the reader's advocate, particularly the reader who would place themselves in the "non-techie" category. She caused my writing to improve, and ultimately became a writing collaborator at the end as we strove to get everything just right.

I also have to give a shout out to my son-in-law Dave Thomas (affectionately known as *The Dave Thomas*). He's the engineer in the family, and was instrumental in guiding us through the wacky world of how Apple deals with photos.

My family is awesome - Thank you!

Table of Contents

Introduction

Welcome to this exciting new book devoted to turning your mobile device into a genealogy powerhouse. This started out as a second edition to *Turn Your iPad into a Genealogy Powerhouse*. Since it is nearly a complete rewrite (a lot has changed in the last few years!) and now covers Apple and Android, it really is its own book. The goal of the book remains the same: setting you up for genealogical success and squeezing every last opportunity out of the investment you made in your mobile device.

And of course I'm saying "mobile device" because there are now so many different options available. Even if I were just to focus on the iPad, we would have several generations (and sizes) to address.

This book is much more versatile than its predecessor. You will find it valuable whether you have an Apple or an Android, a tablet or a smartphone, or some combination. We'll talk about that more after I tell you my story.

This is the story I told in the first edition of this book, detailing my introduction to mobile computing and specifically the iPad (though it could have just as easily been about an Android). I retell it here because it may be very similar to your story, and I want new readers to know my past before we launch into the future.

Did you just buy the most expensive email checker EVER?!

Ever since Apple announced the original iPad I had my eye on it. Everyone was going mobile, and smart phones were all the rage in 2010 (which seems like ages ago technologically speaking). But with a screen measuring just slightly bigger than a credit card, it's just not large enough for most of us over 40 to see.

In April 2010 Apple released the iPad in all its 9.7-inch diagonal glory, and for the first time I could imagine hitting the road without my laptop.

Then my husband heard about my plans.

"You know they are just going to release a new one in a year. You need to wait," he sensibly advised.

Sensibility and patience are two traits I lack when it comes to electronic gadgets. However, with a base price tag of $499 for the 16GB Wi-Fi version, this was a significant purchase. In my heart I knew he was right, so I waited.

When the iPad 2 was finally announced in March 2011 it was as if the starting flag had dropped, and I placed my pre-order online. iPad 2 was worth the wait, being about 33% thinner and 15% lighter than its predecessor. It also sported a better processor that Apple boasted was much faster. My husband's a pretty smart guy.

When it finally arrived I played around with some of the apps it came loaded with, and then downloaded a few more. I went to play a video on this gorgeous color display, only to discover it didn't support Adobe Flash, which has been a program essential for viewing a large percentage of online videos. Eventually I found myself just playing Angry Birds, wondering what I was going to do with it.

As I sat on the couch and flung yet another pudgy red cardinal at a pile of pigs my husband walked by and asked, "Did you just buy the most expensive email checker EVER?"

At that moment my mission became clear: Figure out how to make this amazing piece of hardware a genealogy workhorse!

My first step was to determine what I thought I wanted to do with my iPad. I say thought, because it's clear that my expectations have changed as I have become more familiar with the tablet, and it has many capabilities I never knew I needed.

Next, I needed to climb out of the genealogy box and into the online technology world to learn more about the direction of mobile computing and the role that tablets are playing. So I put on my genealogy cap, and looked at the larger tech community's offerings and insights, all the time keeping our family history needs in mind.

And finally I have put my money where my mouth is. I have embraced every opportunity to turn to my iPad first, before pulling out the laptop, or scrounging through my cavernous purse for my cell phone. Necessity is the mother of invention, and there's nothing more motivating for figuring out how your iPad can meet a need than when you are in a crunch or under a deadline.

The result of these activities over the last year is that this little silver darling has happily weaseled its way into nearly every aspect of my life.

In genealogical terms I snap, edit, catalogue, and share family photos, record interviews, take endless notes, grab pieces of content off family history websites, find the closest library, create heirloom catalogues, listen to podcasts, watch videos, keep up on genealogy news, navigate genealogy conferences, document graves, and so much more!

In business terms I take credit card payments, manage the Genealogy Gems official Facebook page, tweet on Twitter, view and analyze podcast listener statistics, record interviews, snap photos and videos, take notes, write books, plan my speaking engagement trips, and even video-call my grandson or husband for a quick chat from my hotel room.

And of course the move into my personal life was easy. It sits on the kitchen counter providing me with recipes to follow, podcasts to listen to, TV and movies to watch, and books to read. I play learning games with my grandson, and even make recordings of me reading an iPad book that he can play at night on his daddy's iPad before he goes to bed. With my iPad I shop, doodle, and

Genealogy

even play games when I have a spare moment.

Yes, this pound and a half of aluminum, scratch-resistant glass and itsy bitsy computer components has fit nicely into my busy life. After reading this book, the iPad (or other brand tablet) will become an indispensable part of your genealogy toolkit.

A lot has changed since I originally penned this story. The iPad and iPhone are available in an ever growing number of sizes, and with each iteration, they have new features and capabilities. This complicates things for your humble author who wants to help you get the most out of your mobile device, whatever it may be. And it may be an Android.

Android is certainly giving Apple a run for its money in the U.S. as illustrated by the recent article on Gigaom.com declaring "Android and iOS are nearly tied for U.S. smartphone market." And worldwide, it's not much of a contest as the Business Insider declared: "In Q4 2013, according to research firm IDC, Google's Android mobile operating system had a 78% share of all users globally." If you're like me, you may very well have both an Apple device and an Android!

What does all this mean for you and me and this new book? I will cover that in the next section.

A Few Tips for Using this Book

As I said, the mobile market is changing quickly, and that means it is time for an all new book. First, you'll notice that the title has changed to reflect that this book will include the growing variety of mobile devices available. It's not just about the iPad anymore! This book applies to tablets and smart phones (which are essentially small tablets these days), as well as Apple's iOS and Android.

Even though we are tackling a more diversified playing field, I will do my best to keep this book an easy read that will get you up and running quickly. As you read, please keep in mind that when I say "tablet" or "mobile device" I'm talking about all types of mobile devices including smartphones. And that leads us to your job:

Know your mobile device.

In the case of an iPad for example, what this means is that you will need to know which generation iPad you have (1st, 2nd, 3rd, 4th, Air, Pro, etc.).

You'll also want to ensure that your device is updated to the most current operating system available.

How to find the version of your operating system:

1. Tap Settings

2. Tap General (iOS) or About Device (Android)

3. Tap Software Update

4. You will either see that your operating system software is up to date (and what version it currently is), or you will be notified it is out of date and prompted to update it.

No matter which device and platform you are using, focus on the concepts I present. These will serve you well regardless of which device I use in a specific example. When in doubt if your device can accomplish what I've described, turn to Google. A few quick Google searches should provide the alternatives available to the apps and techniques I discuss here, and clarify whether or not your particular device supports it.

Also, if you're sure that your device does support a particular functionality, but it doesn't work when you try it, that's an indication that you need to check your Settings. Some functionality requires that activation in the Settings. So before you declare your device broken or toss this book in the garbage, take a deep breath and head to the Settings. I will also do my best to indicate when a Setting requires activation along the way.

My job is to provide what I think are the most valuable and universal (usable by the most readers possible with all your different mobile devices) apps and techniques. That means sometimes you are going to read about a super cool feature only to find your generation of device doesn't support it. However, I think reading about these features is still of value to you because it will keep you up to date as to what is available, and help you make choices about when the time is right to upgrade. I hope you agree.

And finally, as with all my books focused on technology, the guiding principle is:

Everything is Subject to Change!

I'm no more excited about random changes than you are. However, the good news is that many of the changes that technology companies make to improve profitability also improve technology. And those changes tend to build on what you already know.

Not long ago I gave a presentation on using the iPad for genealogy at a national genealogy conference. As I always do, I conducted a quick run through of the material the week before my presentation to ensure that everything in my PowerPoint slides reflected the most current and accurate information. By the time I hit the stage some of the apps were removed from the App Store or revamped, and as usual, a few of the websites I referred to had changed their URL addresses. That could very well happen here. But again, Google is your friend in these situations, and a quick search should provide updated answers and website links.

I often think of the signs I saw posted in London while I was speaking at the *Who Do You Think You Are? Live* conference that said, "Keep Calm and Carry On." These were originally issued by the government in the UK in 1939 to keep up the spirits of the citizenry in the event of invasion. Here's my variation:

We have our work cut out for us, but it is a worthwhile adventure to go on. So let's get going!

Part One: Getting Started

Chapter 1: The Tablet Mindset

If after purchasing your tablet you become frustrated that it doesn't work like a laptop, I want to let you in on a little secret: tablets are not laptops. Breathe deep and let that idea go.

Rather than trying to duplicate what you do on a laptop, the key to success is adopting what I call a "tablet mindset." Think of it this way: even though both a fax machine and computer email can send the same information, you don't use them the same way. You don't shove paper into your computer disc drive to send a message by email, and you don't type your message into the keyboard on the fax machine. This concept also applies to tablets and laptops.

The Cloud

While laptops use software, the tablet leans on apps and Cloud access to get jobs done.

"The Cloud" just means that you use the internet to send your data to be stored, managed and processed by "remote servers" (which are just big computers that are in a different physical location.) This makes a lot of sense for mobile devices because they have limited storage space.

On a laptop you organize your files into folders on your hard drive. While tablets do have memory storage, they are designed to have the bulk of your files organized and stored on the Cloud using apps (which we will discuss in later chapters).

While the tablet looks like a small version of your computer, trying to translate the user approach from PC to tablet just complicates things. Leave PC computing behind, and embrace a new *Tablet Mindset.*

Tablet Mindset Guidelines

- Use apps to accomplish tasks
- Store files on a Cloud-based service
- Access desired content through Cloud-based services (no disk drive here!)
- Go online strictly with Wi-Fi or a service plan
- Take it EVERYWHERE

This short list paints a picture of a computing device that is clearly a different animal from your desktop computer!

In the following chapters we will dig deeper into these areas and I'll share with you step by step instructions to get the most out of your tablet.

The Tablet Mindset remains the cornerstone of my approach in this book. But now that we have a few years of tablet use under our belt, I want to introduce you to an additional concept that will reduce frustration today and take you into the future.

App Consolidation

It's the idea that more is not necessarily better when it comes to mobile apps.

Just the other day I saw a website article suggesting 50 productivity apps (Ammouth, Doug "50 Free Apps to Make You an Incredibly Productive Person" Fast Company, Mansueto Ventures, LLC, 16 October 2015). If I need 50 apps to be productive I'm just going to set my tablet down and take a nap. Think of the hours it would take to locate, download, organize and learn to use those 50 apps.

Now maybe they didn't really mean that we should all use 50 apps to be productive, but we all know folks who have huge numbers of apps on their tablet. Maybe even you do. The number is often so large that we can spend as much time looking for the app as using them.

Take a minute right now, set down this book, and take a look at what you're carting around on your device. Do you see apps that you thought looked cool but now sit on your home screen taking up space and battery resources? Delete them! Don't worry. They will still be in the App store under "Purchased" waiting patiently in the Cloud for you to download them again any time. Hopefully after reading this book, you won't need most of them. If you need an incentive to do this, head to your Settings and look at your storage usage number.

Apple: Settings > General > Storage and iCloud Usage

Android: Settings > Data Usage

(See image next page)

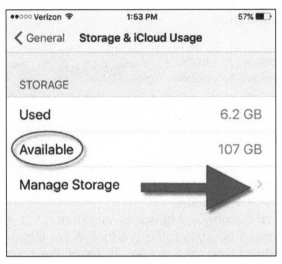

Make a note of it. Then go and delete those apps you aren't using and probably never will. When you go back to see your storage usage number, you may be pleasantly surprised at how much space you freed up! It's a good habit to do this regularly. Now you've got more space for some of the awesome apps I'm going to tell you about in this book.

The truth is it's not that hard for a motivated programmer to create an app that does one basic task, so there are tons of them out there. However, if I was discussing computer software programs and suggesting that you buy a program for each task, you would laugh – and rightly so! Let's demand more from our apps and devices, and focus on carefully selecting and investing in the apps that can consolidate our efforts and tasks. There are some real workhorses out there and we're going to lasso them.

Chapter 2: Genealogy Task Wish List

It's tempting to sit down with your tablet, head to the app store, and just search for the word "genealogy." Resist the temptation (and save yourself some money and disappointment). Rather than let the app store (and the apps you stumble into) dictate what you can do, start by making a wish list. Ask yourself: What would I like to be able to do genealogically with my tablet? The sky is the limit!

Here's what my genealogy task wish list looked like when I got my first tablet:

- View my family tree from my genealogy software database
- Update my genealogy software database and synchronize the data with my home computer
- Take written research notes
- Take digital images of documents
- Record oral history interviews
- Work on websites
- Easily retrieve websites (i.e. bookmark)
- Copy information from websites
- Take, edit and share photos
- Create captivating family history projects that I can share easily
- Conduct location-based research (Google Earth)
- Get ongoing genealogical education (blogs, podcasts, magazines, etc.)

- Watch videos
- Manage family history projects
- Make audio and video phone calls while on research trips
- Read and annotate eBooks
- Continue to collaborate with other researchers
- Keep things organized
- And yes, even check my email

Of course, I am limited by my current understanding of what I might wish to do.

'Update my genealogy software database and sync with my home computer' is an example of something that may not be currently possible with all genealogy database programs. However, this capability may very well be widely available within weeks of this book coming out. In fact, that's one of the challenges in writing and speaking about technology – things are moving at lightning speed. What we discuss here could change tomorrow. But if you understand the concepts, you can adjust accordingly.

I can't over-emphasize the importance of when I say "I am limited by my current understanding of what I might wish to do." I want you to keep this thought in the back of your mind as you read the book and work with your mobile device. Let me give an example of why I believe this is so important. When I got my iPad, one item that I didn't put on my list because I simply didn't know it was possible, was to access and run my home computer remotely. When I heard about this capability my iPad made the leap from helpful, to indispensable. (In this book we will cover what your options are and how to use remote access.)

Another capability fell in my lap at a genealogy conference a few years ago. My daughter and I were sitting at my Genealogy Gems booth in Loveland, Colorado and had customers lining up to buy my book *The Genealogist's Google Toolbox*, and my *Google Earth for Genealogy* video series. They were full of excitement having just witnessed what Google's technology could do for them in class. As they approached the table, credit card in hand, their faces dropped when we repeated our mantra, "Sorry we can't accept credit cards. We can take cash or checks." These days most people have to reach back in to the recesses of their memories to recall what a check is, and in the end they would sacrifice their cash lunch money.

We didn't like having to break the 'no credit card' news. But being a small business we just weren't in a position to sign up with a major bank to process credit cards when our in-person sales occur sporadically at conferences.

A fellow conference vendor heard our speech and came over after the next class session began and the crowds thinned. He asked me if I had an iPad and I proudly said yes. "Good, then you can accept credit cards!" he announced.

Within about 10 minutes he set up a Square account for us, and downloaded the free app. Sales nearly doubled for the rest of the conference as we happily met our customer's needs and accepted their plastic.

Squareup has revolutionized small businesses in the blink of an eye by making credit card acceptance easy and affordable for everyone. PayPal now offers its own Pay Here app and credit card swiping device. Competition is a beautiful thing and should only serve to enhance the features we receive as end users.

Are you a member of a genealogy society? Consider the possibilities of being able to accept credit card payments at meetings and conferences for the books your group publishes, registration fees, and other products that help financially support the organization.

So don't be afraid to dream. Make your list now and through this book we will set up most of what you want right away. As for the rest, don't worry, it's probably right around the next technological corner.

Part Two: The Apps

Chapter 3: There's an App for That!

Now that you have a starting list of genealogical tasks you want to accomplish, it's time to download the apps that can fulfill your mission. We'll head to Apple's App Store first and then move on to Google Play.

App Store

You'll find your iPad comes ready loaded with the App Store app. Tap the icon to open up a world of apps – well over one million and counting!

Currently the menu is across the bottom of the app. There you'll find tabs for:

Featured

This section is all about just what it says. This is where the App Store promotes new and "noteworthy" apps. The Featured section is definitely fun to browse when you have spare time, but you're not likely to find genealogy specific apps there.

Top Charts

Here you'll find the most popular free and paid apps. This represents what mobile users at large are using the most. You can also filter the list and see the top apps in each category.

Explore

Explore recommends apps by categories. No, you won't find a "genealogy" category listed, but then again, we don't need one. Our Tablet Mindset is geared to the category model, so this is an easy and worthwhile place to navigate around the store. Categories such as Books, Business, Education, Lifestyle, Photo & Video, Productivity, Reference, and Utilities will be of particular interest to genealogists and the tasks we face. Each category has subsets. For example, the Lifestyle category includes Family and you'll find genealogy apps in the Popular section. My favorite category is definitely Productivity, which speaks to accomplishing tasks. Within Productivity you'll find loads of subset categories that you'll want to dig into!

You can skip browsing all together and target your searches by tapping the Search icon and using the search box.

Purchased

Here you'll find a listing of all your apps, as well as tools for remembering your Apple account password, redeeming gift cards and getting online support help. Purchased is found in the bottom menu on the iPad, and in Updates on the iPhone.

According to Apple: *Your apps in iCloud.* "When you buy and download apps from the App Store, you always have access to them, no matter which device you're using, because the App Store keeps them in the cloud. So if you bought an app on your iPhone, it can automatically download straight to your iPad over Wi-Fi or 3G and vice versa. And if you delete an app from your device, you can always download it again."

Updates

One thing about apps is that they seem to be constantly updated, which is actually a good thing as it often means the developers are working out the bugs and adding new features. Periodically check the Updates area to update individual apps, or avail yourself of the Update All button to get it done in one fell swoop.

A balloon will appear on your App Store app icon, displaying the number of your apps that currently have updates available for download. Tap Updates to see your Pending Updates as well as updates that you have initiated or that were updated automatically in recent days.

Keep in mind that while an app is updating it is not available for use. I made the mistake once of seeing that an app had an available update and thought I would just tap it before using it for an urgent need (like snapping a photo of a genealogical document.) It seemed like an eternity passed before it was up and running again and I could get back to work. In reality it was probably only a minute or so, but you get the idea.

Categories

(Upper left corner of the store when viewing Featured or Top Charts) In this section apps are broken up into commonly searched featured categories. While you won't find "genealogy" or "history" in the list, categories that are worth perusing for apps to meet wish list needs include Navigation, Photo & Video, Productivity, Reference, Social Networking, and Utilities.

Wish List

Have you ever discovered an app that looks promising but has a price tag that you're not sure you want to pay? Now you can save apps to your Wish List and continue your app search for alternatives before making a purchase.

How to add an app to your Wish List:

1. Tap an app in the App Store
2. Tap the Share icon
3. Tap Add to Wish List
4. To review your Wish List, tap the List icon at the top of the Featured, Top Charts, Explore, or Purchased screens.

Unfortunately, as of this writing, you can't add free apps to your Wish List for future reference.

Google Play Store

When Google finally entered the tablet playing field with the Nexus 7 in the summer of 2012, it was on the heels of a conversion of the Android Marketplace into Google Play. While you will now find over a million apps in the Google Play Store, they are not all optimized for tablets. However, that will change very rapidly, and rest assured you'll be seeing updates.

As I stated earlier, I've placed a priority on identifying quality apps with a universal appeal (both Apple and Android) However, the origins of this book was a focus on the iPad, so in the app section you may find a few apps that are only for the iPad. I will always strive to provide an Android counterpart.

The Google Play store combines apps along with Games, Movies & TV, Music, Books, and Newsstand. Since our focus is Apps, tap Apps.

The menu across the top will help you navigate the App section of Google Play. Here you'll find self-explanatory tabs: Categories, Home, Top Paid, Top Free, Top Grossing, and Top New Paid.

For efficient browsing, tap Categories. Of particular interest to us will be categories such as:

- Books & Reference
- Communication
- Education
- Family
- Media & Video
- Photography
- Productivity (my favorite)
- Tools
- Travel & Local

(Ah, you probably noticed I skipped Libraries & Demos. Sorry all you genealogists, they're not talking about our kind of libraries!)

For more targeted searching, use the search box found at the top of every screen. Tap the microphone icon to speak your query.

The Menu

The Menu icon is in the upper left corner of your screen. (Note: As you dig into app browsing you'll need to tap the Back arrow to return to a top level page in order to access it.) You will have signed into your Google account and will see your user name. Here you'll have quick access to:

The Store home page

My Apps

Tap the Installed apps to see all the apps you have currently installed. This is where you'll update them individually or with the Update All button.

Tap the All tab to see all the apps you have purchased, whether they are currently installed or not.

My Wishlist

Adding apps to your wishlist is easy and flexible. While browsing apps you can quickly add apps to your wishlist.

Simply tap the Share (3 dots) icon and then tap Add to wishlist. In addition, each app has a wishlist icon (the ribbon with the plus sign) on its product page. Tap it and it's added.

How to access your wishlist in Google Play:

1. Tap Menu

2. Tap *My Wishlist*

3. Tap an item in your wishlist to visit its detail page to install, purchase, or remove it from your wishlist

People

This is where Google taps into its strength: your global Google account. In the People section you'll find the friends you have connected with through your Google account and see activity and reviews.

My Account

Here you can manage your payment methods, subscriptions, rewards, and order history.

Staying Up to Date - App Resources

In doing research for this book, I was reminded how fast the tablet and app markets have grown. The Geeknaut website at www.geeknaut.com sports a chart that shows the meteoric growth in app downloads. The chart shows that in March 2009 there were 2,300 apps in the Android Marketplace (now Google Play Store). By August of 2010 that number had jumped to 80,000 apps that had been downloaded 1 billion times. By December 2011 apps had reached nearly 400,000 apps and a total of 10 billion downloads! Today we're talking apps in the millions.

These staggering numbers are one of the reasons I wrote this book. You don't need all the available apps...you just need the best ones to accomplish the tasks at hand. The focus of the apps listed here is genealogy, but you will likely have other business and personal things you want to do. There are some great apps and websites that will help you cut through all the app noise and get to the things you really need.

Apple App Resources

BestAppSite

www.Bestappsite.com

(iOS) The purpose of this website is all in the name. The folks at BestAppSite review what they consider the best apps that they find on the App Store. You'll find convenient app lists to help you zero in on the type of app you need. You'll also find helpful how-to guides on using your iPad.

App Advice

www.appadvice.com

(iOS) This website is also available as an app for $1.99. Be sure to check out the App Lists. AppAdvice does a great job with these and is a well-respected resource. I couldn't be more proud of the fact that the Genealogy Gems Podcast app made the iPad Apps for Hobbyists list as a "must have" app.

Also at the bottom of the screen you'll find AppGuides. This section falls right in line with my App Consolidation concept.

AppAdvice acknowledges that there are probably 10 different apps for each type of task you want to accomplish, and their goal, much like in this book, is to bring you the best and help you select one that will do the job.

Apps are grouped by type. For instance, under Productivity you can review their grouping of apps strictly devoted to handwriting for the iPad. AppAdvice strives to do the homework for you and, provides you with quick reviews that get to the heart of the apps strengths and weaknesses.

Are you looking for a particular type of app? The search box on the website is invaluable for using keywords to dig up a great app.

Android App Resources

Android Pit

www.androidpit.com

Click the Apps tab to go straight to the app reviews and recommendations. But don't miss the Tips and Tricks tab for answers to your Android questions. If you're in a hurry, click the magnifying glass in the top right corner of the home page to search the website.

Android Authority

www.androidauthority.com

Much like Android Pit, Android Authority offers up News, Reviews, and Apps. In addition you'll find a handy main menu (that looks just like the Android menu icon) in the upper left corner loaded with more quick links. Don't miss the Android Security section under Features for tips on how to improve your privacy on Android.

My Picks

Speaking of picking the best apps, let's get right to my picks for the best apps for you, the genealogist.

Falling in line with our *Genealogists Task Wish List* in chapter 2, I have organized these apps into "Task Categories" based on the tasks they accomplish. Of course, some apps fall under multiple categories.

All of these apps are available on the App Store. I have also made an effort to identify the Android counterparts. When a particular app is not available on Google Play I have offered a similar alternative when available. However, I have opted not to include an alternative when the alternatives have poor ratings or I don't feel they are worthy of inclusion.

And of course the obligatory disclaimer

As with everything else in life, it's up to you to do your own due diligence. Read app descriptions carefully. I am happy to share apps I have had positive experiences with, but understand that you always download at your own risk.

One More Note about Apps

While it is optimum to find an iPad version of an app when you are working on an iPad, it's not mandatory. For example, some of the apps I list in this book are actually iPhone and not iPad apps. That's OK. The important thing is that it can accomplish the task at hand.

If you search the App Store for a particular app and don't find what you are looking for, try tapping the dropdown arrow next to "iPad Only" in the top left corner and select "iPhone Only." The store will then display results for iPhone apps.

When you open an iPhone app on the iPad it will appear the size of an iPhone on the iPad screen. To expand an iPhone app to fill the ample iPad screen, touch the "2x" button in the bottom right corner of the app window. While you may find the app images are not quite as sharp as images featured in apps specifically created for the iPad, they will still be quite functional.

Chapter 4: Browsing

When it comes to web browsers, chances are you will gravitate to the browser that is native to your device:

Apple: Safari

Android: Google Chrome

All share common strengths but there are some differences. Depending on how you like to surf the web, you may want to consider going with a different browser. In the interest of "app consolidation" you only need one, although nothing is to say you can't have all three. And yes, there are three browsers I am going to highlight: the two native browsers and an exception free browser that I think you'll love as much as I do.

Safari

by Apple

Price: Free

Available: included with Apple device

Safari is Apple's web browser that comes preinstalled on Apple devices. One upside to using Safari is that you can sync your bookmarks and open tabs across all of your iCloud connected devices. Let's take a look at some of the best features.

Search

Although Safari is a web browser, the address field is now also your search engine.

How to conduct a search of the web:

1. Tap the address field at the top of the screen (icons for Bing, Yahoo, Google and Apple appear as options, but Google is set by default.)

2. Type in your search query, or save time and tap the microphone button in the keyboard that pops up and speak your query.

3. Tap the Go button in the keyboard

You can change up your search experience in Settings > Safari > Search. Tap Search Engine and you can change the default search engine from Google to Yahoo, Bing or DuckDuckGo. You'll also find on/off slider buttons for Search Engine Suggestions, Safari Suggestions, and Preload Top Hit.

Safari Save

If you find a photograph on a website while using the Safari browser, saving a copy of it is a snap:

1. Press and hold your finger on the image
2. Select "Save Image" from the pop up menu
3. This will save the image to your camera roll which you can access through the Photos app

Word Search

Safari's ability to find a word on a page is bit hidden, but easy to use once you find it.

How to search for a word or phrase while viewing a website:

1. Tap the address bar at the top of the page

2. Type the word you are looking for

3. Tap the Find option under On This Page at the bottom of the list. If you don't see this option, scroll down — it may be obscured by the on-screen keyboard.

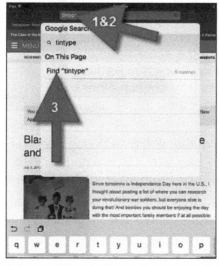

The results will be highlighted on the page for easy review. Tap the up and down arrows at the bottom of the page in the grey bar to scroll through them. You'll see the targeted word in the search field. You can replace that word for a new word or phrase for further searching on the page.

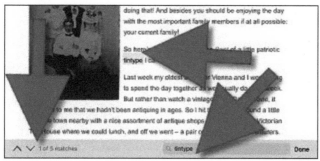

Tabs

If you like to multi-task while you surf the web, then you'll be happy to discover that Safari allows you to open multiple tabs. Tabs are particularly convenient when you want to compare information on a variety of websites. It can also be handy to jump to a new tab in order to quickly reference another website while not losing your place on the first website.

To launch a new tab, tap the plus sign at the top of the screen (tablet) or tap the tabs icon which looks like pages stacked on top of each other, and then tap the plus sign (smartphone).

This will open a blank tab featuring the websites you visit frequently. (You can turn this Frequently Visited Websites off in Settings > Safari > Frequently Visited Sites.)

A convenient function that is not obvious in Safari is the ability to reopen a recently closed tab by pressing and holding the + button.

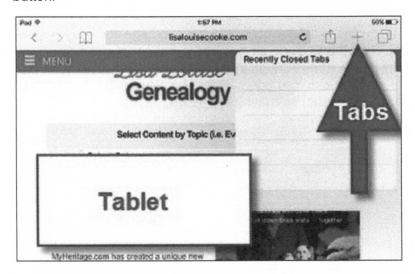

Keyboard Tip

Here's a time-saving Safari tip. When you type a website URL directly into the address bar in Safari you don't have to type in ".com" or ".net". Instead, tap and hold the period "." Key. A pop-up balloon will reveal a series of shortcuts, from ".com" to ".us".

Chrome

by Google

Price: Free

Available: App Store, Google Play

Google's Chrome web browser is similar to Safari, and is native to Android devices. Tap the menu (three vertical dots) icon at the top of the screen to explore an assortment of features. Tap Settings to gain a wide array of options for customizing your browsing experience.

Going Incognito

One of the newest and noteworthy features is the Incognito Tab found within the menu. If you are not a fan of Google Chrome saving a record of the websites you visit and download, incognito mode is for you. Any searching from within that tab will not be saved to history.

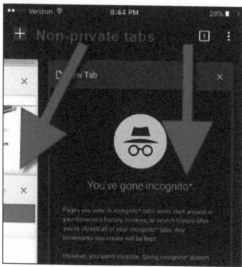

Keep in mind that if your computing device is tied into your employer or other organization that has provided you with the device, you are not invisible to them. That includes your internet service provider.

Also, you must close all incognito* tabs in order to clear cookies.

Voice Search

Since Chrome is by Google, it's not a surprise to find the popular Google search engine built in. But typing your search query, particularly on the relatively small screen of a smartphone, can be challenging. Chrome takes advantage of your device's built-in microphone for hands free searching. Tap the microphone icon in the address bar. A red circle with a microphone will appear and you'll hear a "ding". Speak your query, and Google will type the query on the screen. When you stop talking it will automatically run the search for you.

Some search results will also include a voice response. When Google is telling you about the results, you will see that the microphone icon changes into a speaker icon.

Find in Page

You can also save time in your research by using the "find in page" feature to find desired words and phrases.

How to find text on a page:

1. Tap menu (three dots icon)
2. Tap Find in Page
3. Type the word or phrase in the "Find in Page" field that appears
4. As soon as you stop typing it will show you the occurrences of the word highlighted on the page

5. Tap the up and down arrows to scroll through the occurrences

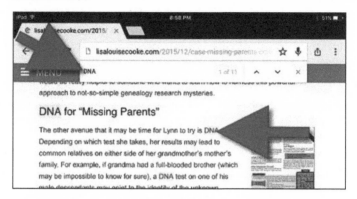

6. Tap the X in the Find in Page field to cancel the search feature.

Google

by Google

Price: Free

Available: App Store, Google Play

This is Google's dedicated search app. The beauty of this app is that you can set it up to be hands free!

To get going, tap the microphone button and "allow" it permission to access your device's microphone. From that point forward, all you have to do is say "OK Google" and speak your search query. No more tapping the microphone. Every step saved is more time spent researching.

This is one of those features that my first reaction is "that's not a big deal." But *it is a big deal.* It's convenient in a big way. After just a couple of searches you'll love it like I do.

Dolphin

by: MoboTap Inc.

Price: Free

Available: App Store, Google Play

The one thing we probably do more than anything else on our tablet is surf the web. While your first instinct on an iPad would be to use Apple's web browser Safari, and on the Android Google's Chrome, I propose there is a better way to browse. Dolphin is one of the most powerful web browsing apps available, and it is free.

The folks at Dolphin are keenly aware that there is much more to accessing websites than just typing in a URL. And in fact with Dolphin you don't even have to type in the address to access a website.

Gestures

Dolphin's "Gestures" feature saves you browsing time by letting you program a simple drawn "gesture" that links to any website you regularly use. You can also set up gestures to execute regular tasks you do on a browser such as open a new tab.

To get started, tap the "pointing hand" icon, then tap the Gear icon on the pop-up window to see available default gestures. These include:

- Go to Bottom and Go to Top (of the page)
- New (web browser) Tab
- Launching a few popular websites such as Google

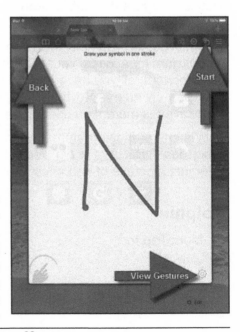

Let's give one of these a try. Tap *New Tab*. On the next screen you'll see an example of the drawn gesture, the letter "N".

As you can see, the gesture was drawn in one continuous stroke. This is the key to creating and executing gestures. Tap the back arrow until you get back to the blank gestures screen, and draw

a capital "N" in one continuous stroke

When you release the stroke a new tab will open ready for browsing the web. Multiple tabs allow you to multi-task your web browsing. Tap the desired tab to jump between web pages.

Take gestures to the next level by creating custom gestures for the websites you visit most often. Here are some of my gestures:

How to add a custom gesture:

1. Tap the "pointing hand" icon
2. Tap the gear icon
3. Tap + Create Gesture
4. Type or paste in the URL address you want the gesture to navigate to.
5. Tap Next
6. In one stroke draw the desired gesture. (i.e. "f" for www.familysearch.org)
7. Tap Save

Alternative way to add a custom gesture:

1. Navigate to a web page
2. Tap the plus sign (+) next to the URL address
3. Tap Add Gesture
4. Draw a one-stroke gesture
5. Tap Save

You can also delete gestures and revise the drawing that represents the gesture.

How to delete a gesture:

1. Tap the gestures icon
2. Tap the gear icon
3. Tap Edit
4. Tap the minus sign next to the gesture you wish to delete
5. Tap Delete
6. Tap Done

How to edit a gesture:

1. Tap the gestures icon
2. Tap the gear icon
3. Tap the gesture you want to edit
4. Tap "Better draw the pattern in one stroke"

5. Draw the new gesture

6. Tap Save

Find on Page

Another excellent feature for the genealogist is Find on Page. When you land on a lengthy page, Find on Page can speed up the process for locating the information you seek.

How to find text in Dolphin:

1. Tap three 3 horizontal lines icon at top browser bar

2. Tap Find on Page

3. Type in a word or phrase (or tap the microphone key to dictate)

4. Tap Search on Keyboard

5. Occurrences of that word or phrase will be highlighted on the page

6. Tap the arrows at the bottom of the screen to move to each occurrence

7. When you're done, tap the X to the left of the Find box at the bottom of the screen

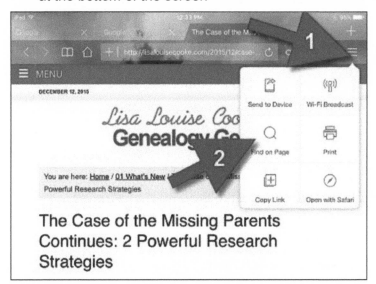

Additional tools found within the three horizontal line icon are:

- *Send to Device* (this allows Dolphin to connect to your other devices and synchronize web content.)

- *W-Fi Broadcast* (Collaborating with others? This tool allows you to share and receive webpages from folks nearby)

- *Print* (Connect with AirPrint printers)

- *Copy Link* (copies the URL to your device's clipboard so it can be pasted elsewhere)

- *Open with Safari*

Speed Dial

Here's another way to save time and quickly jump to your favorite genealogy websites. It's called Speed Dial, and they are essentially book mark icons that appear on the home screen. You'll find some already set up for you by tapping the Home icon (the house to the left of the address bar at the top of the screen).

You may not want all of the default Speed Dial buttons, so let's clear them out of the way.

How to remove unwanted speed dial buttons:

1. Tap Home
2. Tap Edit (bottom of the screen) OR press and hold the button you want to delete
3. Tap the X next to the unwanted button
4. In the pop up dialog box tap Delete
5. Tap Done

Now you are ready to add your own custom Speed Dial buttons. There are two ways to do this.

How to add custom speed dial buttons - Method #1:

1. Navigate to the desired website
2. Tap the + plus button on the address bar
3. Tap Add Speed Dial
4. In the pop up dialog box edit the name of the Speed Dial as desired

5. Tap Save

6. Tap Home and you will see your Speed Dial button has been added.

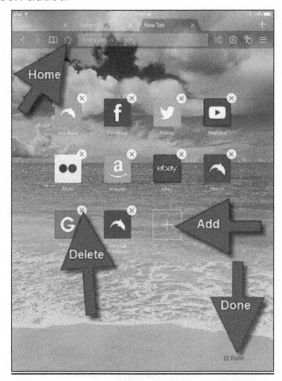

How to add custom speed dial buttons - Method #2:

1. Tap the Home icon

2. Tap the + Plus button

3. In the pop up dialog box Type in the name of the website and the URL

4. Tap Save

5. Tap Home and you will see your Speed Dial button has been added.

The final step is to organize your speed dials. Press and hold a Speed Dial button, and then drag and drop it to the desired location. I like to organize them in rows by type:

Row #1: Most used

Row #2 & 3: Genealogy Records Sites

Rows #4: Social Media

Currently you can have up to 15 Speed Dials.

Mobile Web Clipping and Screen Capture

In addition to being a great browser, Dolphin also has an Evernote web clipper built right in. This means that you can save pages, articles, and more from any website to your free Evernote account. (Learn more about Evernote in the Note Taking chapter.)

Start by tapping the Share icon (iOS) or Dolphin icon and then Share (Android) and then tap the Evernote elephant icon. Since many websites are mobile-friendly (providing you with just one article on the screen at a time) you will see that the green button says Save to Article. Tap the down arrow next to the green Save Article button (iOS, although it could be added to Android in the future) and you will also find an option for Save Full Page (both iOS and Android). The area to be saved will be outlined in yellow. Before you tap the Save button, take a moment to title your note, select a notebook if desired, and tag it with the appropriate tags. You can even conveniently add additional comments.

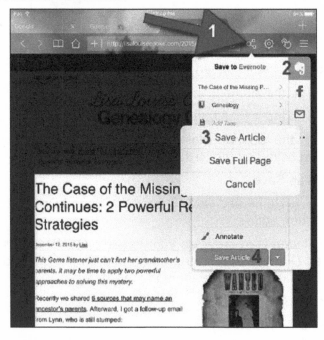

As genealogists though, sometimes we need to do more than just save an item. We want to work with the item itself, and with the Annotation tool in the Evernote clipper you can do just that. Tap Annotate (above the Save button) and use the brush tool to draw circles around important items, cross items out, or anything else that will assist you in your research.

The eraser allows you to rub out any unwanted markings. When you're done just tap Save. You'll then see a thumbnail image of your annotated clipping above the Save button. When you're done, just tap Save and Dolphin will send it over to your Evernote account. (You will need to authorize Dolphin to connect with your Evernote account the first time you use the clipper.)

Also accessible through the Share icon is the ability to share a web page to Facebook (again you will need to authorize this connection) and email as well as access (through the 3 dot icon) to the other standard share options on mobile devices.

And finally, the Gear icon gives you even more control over your mobile browsing experience:

- *Fullscreen mode*
- *Clear Data* (removing search history)
- *Theme* (to set the browsing mood of your choice with a background)
- *Settings*: this one is packaged with all types of goodies. Change the font size in Dolphin, set your default search engine to your favorite, determine if you want links to open in new tabs (yes, Dolphin supports multiple web browsing tabs for your inner multi-tasker!)
- *Set Dolphin to open* with a new tab page upon launch, or where you last left off

Privacy

Private Mode provides you with a way to browse privately. Activate it under the Gear icon to enjoy the following features:

- No browsing history or cookies will be recorded
- Synchronization of your web browsing history with your other devices will be disabled.

- Dolphin will no longer make search suggestions in the URL bar as you type

- Tabs that you have opened will not be saved.

As you can see, the free Dolphin app is a feature-rich app that can save you time, and give you more flexibility as you surf the web for your genealogical research.

Chapter 5: Note Taking

If there is one thing we do a lot of as genealogists, it is taking notes. With a screen keyboard rather than a hardware keyboard you might think this task is limited on mobile devices. Well, think again.

While you could get a wireless keyboard for your tablet (I did, and while it's great for some things, I've been pretty surprised how rarely I use it) I would recommend that you first get familiar with the available note taking apps. Your finger and a simple stylus will serve you well, and you will be amazed at the wide variety of ways you can take and distribute your notes.

Before you go out and buy that keyboard: be sure to spend time in the final chapters where I will give you several tricks for speeding up your typing and even customizing your screen keyboard.

One more thing about note taking - spend some time with your tablet and you'll discover there are a lot more ways to take notes than typing them on a blank screen. I'm providing a few alternatives so that you can select the one best suited to what you are trying to accomplish, and the device that you own. Here you'll find apps that take audio notes, video notes, handwritten notes, notes on PDF documents, and the list goes on. Get ready to take note!

Evernote

by Evernote

Price: Free

Available: App Store, Google Play

If I was able to download only one note taking app, Evernote would be it. It's the app that pretty much everyone can use regardless of device, and the one that can handle just about every kind of note taking. And gone are the days when it was a bit of an ordeal getting items into Evernote from other apps. Thanks to Evernote's popularity, it is a staple in the Share feature of most of the apps we're discussing in this book. More on that in a minute.

Evernote is not just an app, but also a website, and computer desktop software. Note taking is the heart of their business. Evernote's goal is to help you remember EVERYTHING! (Notice an elephant is their logo!)

Is it possible to remember everything? It appears so with Evernote. That's because in addition to making all your typed notes searchable, Evernote scans all your notes clipped from the web, photos, and more with Optical Character Recognition (OCR) enabling them to be instantly retrieved with a keyword search. So rather than organizing in file folders, it's more like throwing all your notes in a pile and then allowing the search tool to pick them out. Use tags to add yet another layer of retrieval to your notes. *(In the image below I searched for the surname "Burket" in the search box and clicked to select a newspaper clipping from the results list. This displays the clipping with the name highlighted.)*

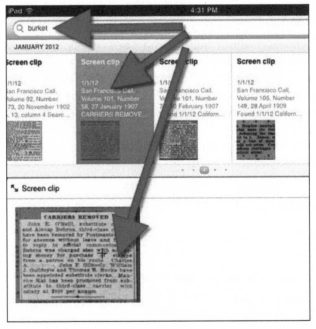

Evernote will keep all your notes (text, screen clips, audio, photos, etc.) organized and backed up on the Cloud so they can be synchronized across all your computing devices. This means your notes move fluidly between Mac and Windows, Apple and Android. Sign up for one free account, and then download the app to your devices and sign in with the same account.

Here are some examples of how I use the Evernote app for genealogy:

Recording podcast and family history interviews

Here's a tip: be sure you don't accidentally cover the built in microphone on your iPad while you hold it during the recording. Yes, this tip is from personal experience! We will talk more about recordings in the upcoming Audio chapter.

Snapping a photo of people I meet at conferences

When I meet someone of note at a conference, I ask the individual to hold up their name badge, and I take a photograph of them with my tablet or phone. Evernote OCRs the photo and I can retrieve it simply by typing a name (word) that appears on the tag. A great way to remember folks!

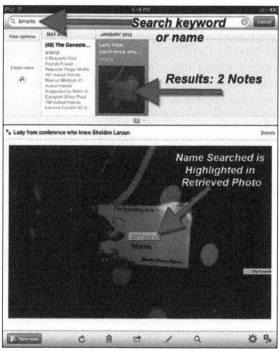

You can now take the photo right from the Evernote app. All you have to do is open the Evernote app, tap the Photos icon, take the photo, and tap Save. The photo will save as a note and with an internet connection OCR will be applied during the synchronization process. No longer do you have to take the photo with your device's camera and then share it to Evernote. It all happens in the app.

Clipping important bits off of genealogy websites

With Evernote, I grab only what I want, which means the image file is smaller and more focused. And I love that I can clip source citation information and include it on the note of the clipped document or data.

Creating an outline for the book I am writing

The predecessor to this book, T*urn Your iPad into a Genealogy Powerhouse*, had its origins in an outline I created in Evernote. I was flying on a plane with no internet connection. As soon as the plane landed, I accessed the internet and opened the app. Evernote automatically synchronized my notes with my laptop and home computer.

Saving newspaper articles I find online

The ability to web clip newspaper articles proved invaluable when I was writing my book *How to Find Your Family History in Newspapers*. Once the images were synchronized through the Evernote servers and OCR'd, I could then retrieve any article by simply typing a keyword into the Evernote search box. Incredible! (See image next page)

I could go on and on about the possibilities, but I think you get the idea.

Web Clipping

If you already use Evernote on your desktop computer then you know how helpful it is to be able to clip and save articles from genealogy websites for future reference. My favorite tool for doing this on my iPad is built into the Dolphin web browser (see the previous Better Browsing chapter). However, sometimes I'm using another browser like Safari or Chrome. Thankfully it is now possible to connect other browsers with Evernote.

How to save a webpage to Evernote (Safari and Chrome)

1. Open the Safari Browser app

2. Navigate to the webpage you want to clip. (Currently on iOS you can only save entire pages. On Android,

however, you can also have the option to press/highlight and clip sections of text in addition to full pages. This could certainly change in the future.)

3. Tap the "Share" icon at the top of the screen

4. Tap Evernote. If you don't see Evernote listed, tap More and slide the lever to activate Evernote. If this is your first time connecting to Evernote you may need to sign in to your account and / or authorize the connection. Just follow the prompts.

5. An Evernote dialog box will appear. Edit the text as desired.

6. Evernote will designate the notebook it thinks is most appropriate for your note. The name of that notebook will appear in the dialog box. Tap the right arrow (Safari) or tap the notebook label (Chrome) to select a different notebook from your list of Evernote notebooks.

7. Tap Save (Safari) or the check mark (Chrome) to close the dialog box. Your note is now saved in Evernote. Go to your Evernote app and you will see it there.

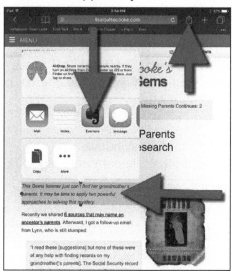

And here's a tip: if you use Evernote frequently, why not move it to first position in the Share list? Just tap Share and press, hold, and drag the Evernote icon so it appears first in your list.

Notes

by Apple

Price: Free

Available: Included with your Apple device

If you have the most current version of iOS, you may have noticed that the Notes app that comes preinstalled has been significantly improved. You can now save attachments to the Notes app such as links, maps, documents and photos. This can be done in any app that shows the share button. Simply tap the share button and then tap Notes. You can also create drawings with your finger or a stylus, and you can make checklists.

Pages

by Apple

Price: Free

Pages has been called "the most beautiful word processor you've ever seen on a mobile device." With Apple's Pages, you can create, edit, and view documents from anywhere.

Pages stores your documents in Apple's iCloud. iCloud then synchronizes the documents with all of your computing devices including PCs with Windows. This gives you access to the most current version of your documents on all of your devices.

How to set up iCloud for Windows:

1. Download iCloud for Windows at https://support.apple.com/en-us/HT204283

2. Restart your computer

3. Make sure iCloud for Windows is open

4. Enter your Apple ID to sign in to iCloud

5. Choose the features and content that you want to keep up to date across your devices

6. Click Apply

In addition to creating and editing documents in Pages, you can even import and edit Microsoft Word documents as well as plain text files.

To get started creating a document in Pages, use one of the 60 Apple-designed templates, or just start with a blank document. Formatting is easy with the many preset styles and fonts. Many of the most important text formatting options are right on your keyboard. Along the top of the keyboard you will find buttons for indentation, font style, font size, alignment, and more.

Save time and dictate your document by tapping the microphone icon next to the space bar on the keyboard. What could be easier!

Microsoft Word

by Microsoft Corporation

Price: Free

Available: App Store (both iPad and iPhone), Google Play

No matter how many apps we use to record information and take notes, there are times when there's no substitute for the old timer on the block: Microsoft Word. Even if you don't personally use Word, chances are at some point someone has sent you valuable information on a Word document. You'll need access to these documents as well on your mobile device, and thankfully, it's easier than ever.

Microsoft now offers free app versions of their Office software including Word, PowerPoint, and Excel. With the Word app you can create, view and edit your documents. The only requirement is that you sign in with a free OneDrive account or with your Office 365 account.

If you don't regularly store your documents in OneDrive you can open documents that are saved to your iPad, documents attached to an email, or in your Dropbox account.

How to connect to your Dropbox account:

1. Tap the Account button at the top left of the screen

2. Tap Add a Service

3. Tap Dropbox

4. Sign in to Dropbox

5. When you go to Open in the menu, your Dropbox account will appear and you can select a document you have saved.

The Microsoft Word app has most of the features you are accustomed to using on your computer. When you edit documents on your tablet or phone, they will look the same wherever you view them. You may add images, charts, and take advantage of the extensive formatting capabilities.

Google Docs

by Google

Price: Free

Available: App Store, Google Play

Google Docs is Google's answer to Microsoft Office. It's a cloud-based solution for creating text documents, spreadsheets, presentations, forms and more. If you have a free Google account, then you've already taken the first step to using Google Docs and it's cohort Google Drive. Learn more at www.google.com/docs/about/.

The Google Docs apps empowers you to create, edit and collaborate with others on documents from your mobile device, unleashing you from your desktop computer. You can create new documents or edit any that were created on the web or on another device. And for those times when you don't have an internet connection there's no need to worry because you can work on your documents without it. One of my favorite features is that Google Docs auto-saves as you work.

And speaking of Office, Google Docs allows you to open, edit and save Microsoft Word documents, save them as Docs, and even export them again as Office files.

Chapter 6: File Storage & Management

Because mobile devices aren't laptops, they typically don't have USB ports to easily plug into other devices to transfer files. And although my Samsung tablet, for example, has an SD card, my iPad has no portable storage options at all. Mobile storage space is also much more limited than a computer's. All of these challenges lead us to the vital importance of file storage and management for our mobile devices.

File storage is pretty straight forward. We need a place to save files that doesn't take up our device's limited storage. Just start taking photos and file storage will soon become an issue. (We will cover that more in depth in the Photography chapter.) Cloud storage is the solution to this challenge, and all of the apps we will be discussing here provide cloud storage. If you need a refresher on "the cloud" head back to the "Tablet Mindset" chapter at the beginning of this book.

The title of this chapter also includes *management*. What I'm talking about here is moving your files. How do we get files from our tablet to our computer and back again? How do we move files between devices? These challenges are also handled by apps that harness the power of the cloud.

In this chapter I will present to you the top apps and services that provide real solutions. After doing my own homework, these are the ones I have chosen to handle my own files. There are others out there, but these are the leaders. If you would rather go with a different app, I trust this chapter will benefit you by familiarizing you with the types of services, features, and storage plans so that you can do your own homework.

Dropbox

by Dropbox

Price: Free

Available: App Store, Google Play

In my opinion, Dropbox is a "must-have" Cloud service and app. Granted, that may be because I was a very early Dropbox user. I've used the free version for years to easily access files from all of my computing devices. But it is the continually enhanced features and it's compatibility with so many of the other apps I use that keep me a devoted user.

The Big Picture

Dropbox provides you with a free and easy way to share files between many of your apps and all your various computing devices.

Benefits

Files can be saved, copied or moved to Dropbox on any of your mobile devices. With an Internet connection, your files are automatically synchronized through the Dropbox servers, making them accessible on all of your devices.

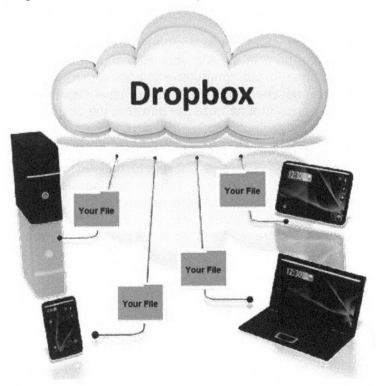

So for example, if you change a file on your tablet, and the tablet is connected to the internet, the file will be updated on the Dropbox servers. Then when you go to your computer, it will be updated as soon as your computer is connected to the internet. If you work on your computer offline and you make changes and resave your document, you won't see the changes on other devices until you have re-connected to the internet and Dropbox has synchronized.

An added benefit of this process is that your files are getting backed up for you on the Dropbox servers. So if you get a new tablet you can easily download the app, sign in to your account and restore all of your files.

Dropbox not only allows you to share links to specific files, but you can also share a link to an entire folder full of content. This is an underutilized strength that could come in handy when you want to share photos, videos and other files with family and friends. And when the file is too large to email, Dropbox handles sharing it like a champ. First let's get you set up with Dropbox.

Getting Started

Start by signing up for a free account at www.dropbox.com, and then install the desktop client version on your computer. You are then ready to download the free app to your tablet, smart phone, etc.

Your Account

Challengers entering the Cloud arena (such as Google Drive) have prompted Dropbox to increase the amount of free storage that you get (now about 2GB). You'll get a lot of mileage out of that. But if you want your storage to be worry-free, there is a fee based version available that serves up a whopping 1TB. You can check how much space you have used at any given time at Settings > Space Used.

Sharing Files

How to share a Dropbox file link:

1. Open the app
2. Tap Files in the menu at the bottom

3. Tap the file you want to share

4. Tap the Share button

5. Tap Email to send the link via email, or Tap Copy Link so that you can paste it in a document or web browser

Recents

A nice time-saving feature of the Dropbox app is Recents. I'll be honest, I used to just ignore Recents. But now that I've upgraded to 1 TB of storage and I've unleashed my usage of Dropbox, I'm finding Recents invaluable for saving time. You probably have files you use often, and with a tap of Recents they are conveniently found in the order you most recently used them, saving you from having to dig through Files.

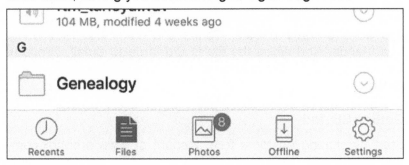

Offline

Saving a file for Offline use makes it easy to access (like a bookmark) by saving the file to your device. Dropbox will attempt to keep the file as up-to-date as possible whenever you are connected to the internet on a Wi-Fi network. According to Dropbox "If you're on a cellular (3G or 4G) network and some files have changed, tap each file to open it and get the latest changes. When on a cellular network, Dropbox will try to spare your data plan. It won't update files unless you tap the Update All button from the Offline files screen."

How to add a file to Dropbox's Offline tab:

1. Tap Files

2. Locate the file you'd like to save offline

3. Tap on the down arrow icon next to the file name (iPad and Android), or three dots (iPhone)

4. Tap Make Available Offline

Once you've made a file available offline, and it has downloaded to your phone or tablet, you'll be able to access it any time by tapping Offline files from the main menu, even if you aren't connected to the internet.

To remove a file from your device that you have downloaded as an Offline File, tap the down arrow next to the file name and tap Remove from Device (or slide the lever on Android.)

Google Drive

by Google, Inc.

Price: Free

Available: App Store, Google Play

Google has added Cloud storage to their list of offerings. Their service is called Google Drive, and it conveniently integrates with Google Docs, their free web-based challenger to Microsoft Office. All together they can make your mobile device a document powerhouse.

Like Dropbox, Google Drive allows you to store your files (photos, documents, videos and other files) so you can access them from any device, and share them with others. Google Drive really shines in the sharing department because you can work on the same master document at the same time, and a log of all the activity is preserved. It's great for collaborating with another genealogist.

So really, this is a two-fer: Google Drive and Google Docs. Both apps are available for free both for Android and for iOS.

The basic plan is free and gives you around 15GB which is plenty of storage to get started. You will find current pricing and storage plans at http://tinyurl.com/DrivePricing.

iCloud

by Apple

Price: Free Apple products. (Upgrade options available for purchase.)

To take advantage of iCloud at www.icloud.com, the first thing you need to do is make sure your Apple device is running the most current iOS (iOS 9 or later).

How to update to the latest version of iOS:

5. Tap Settings

6. Tap General

7. Tap Software Update

8. You will either see that your operating system software is up to date (and what version it currently is), or you will be notified it is out of date and prompted to update it.

Next, you will need to turn on iCloud. Tap the Settings icon on the Home screen, select iCloud, and then enter your Apple ID (the one you use for iTunes.)

Now you are ready to customize your settings. Tap the Settings icon and select iCloud. Tap the On/Off switches to enable the various iCloud services. To activate iCloud Backup, tap Storage & Backup and turn on iCloud Backup.

You can also enable iCloud on your Mac or PC. And like Dropbox and Google Drive you get 5 GB of storage for free, with higher amounts available for a fee.

Chapter 7: Audio

Since my career as a podcaster depends heavily on creating quality interview recordings, I was particularly interested to see what kind of audio my iPad could record and put out. Though you may not be podcasting, as a genealogist it's inevitable that you will find yourself doing scheduled and impromptu interviews with relatives, as well as creating audio notes. Here are some apps that can help you capture those moments both in audio and video formats.

Apple devices come with the Notes app, and Android devices are equipped with the Memo app. Both are easy and intuitive to use. However, only the Android's Memo app records audio. Whether you are using an Apple or an Android, Evernote offers you a reliable option that overcomes the challenges of working with audio from your mobile device beautifully.

Memos

Price: Free

Native to Android

The Memos app offers a super simple way to record audio. And the good news is that it records that audio in a standardized .m4a format that is usable by other programs.

How to record an audio note:

1. Tap the plus sign button
2. Tap Voice and a recording bar will appear at the bottom of the note just above the keyboard
3. Tap the record button (red dot)
4. Press Stop button (square) when done.
5. Tap the Play button to play it back for review
6. Add a text tile and or memo to your note
7. Tape Save

When recording interviews with relatives you may eventually want to include that audio in another project such as a slide show. You will need to send the audio file somewhere where you can retrieve and use it. Emailing a file to yourself is easy enough, although in the case of a very long recording, which results in a large file, you might run into a situation where it's too large to email. A better solution would be to share the file to a free cloud service such as Dropbox, Google Drive, or OneDrive.

How to save an audio file to a Cloud Service:

1. From the main All Memos screen tap the note

2. Tap More

3. Tap Share (from here you can also delete the note)

4. Tap Dropbox or other service

5. Navigate to the folder / location where you want to save the file

6. Tap Add

7. The file will be saved to and accessible from Dropbox

Evernote

by Evernote

Price: Free

Available: App Store, Google Play

The best way I have found to record and organize audio interviews and other recordings is with the Evernote app. There are several reasons why I call it the best when there are other audio recording apps out there:

- *Evernote is cross platform.* It seamlessly synchronizes between Apple and Android, Mac and PC. In a world where you might have a PC at home but an iPhone in your purse, you want to know that your files can be moved easily from one to the other. Evernote handles this synchronization via an Internet connection and requires no conversion of files between platforms.

- *Evernote creates m4a files.* Nothing is worse than using a specialized audio app only to discover that the files created are unique to the app, rendering them useless in other projects. Evernote records in the m4a standardized file format that can be imported into audio editing programs such as Audacity (free) or video editing software such as the free Windows Movie Maker.

- *Evernote keeps your audio notes organized and easily retrievable.* Have you ever saved a file on your computer only to struggle in retrieving it later? Evernote's powerful tagging system and search box make note retrieval a pleasure. We'll discuss this aspect of using Evernote more in depth in the chapter on Notetaking.

How to create an audio note in Evernote:

1. In the app tap the Audio button (iOS) or the plus sign and then the Audio button (Android). (Android Users: If you don't see the Audio / microphone button go to Settings > Notes > Customize + Button. You may only be allowed to select 6 actions that Evernote can do. If Audio is not selected, it will not appear. Tap to add and remove the various actions.)

2. In the new note that pops up, tap the microphone button at the top of the screen.

3. Begin to speak. You will see the wave file at the top, indicating that Evernote is recording.

4. When finished, tap Done.

5. You will see your recording file in a box on the note

6. Add a title for your note, any desired text, and tag appropriately for your use.

7. When done, tap Save (iOS) or the checkmark (Android) to stop recording and save the audio to your note.

8. To listen to your recording, tap the recording file, and it will play back. Then tap Done.

How to extract the audio file for use in another project:

1. On your computer, open Evernote

2. Select the note containing the audio

3. Right-click on the audio file in the note

4. Select Save As and save it to the desired location on your computer

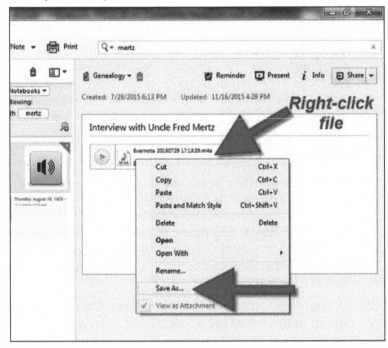

Now you have a saved m4a audio file that can be imported into another program and used to enrich your family history research.

As of this writing the maximum recording length is limited by the total size of the note.

- Basic (free) customers can record up to 25MB per note

- Plus customers can record up to 50MB per note

- Premium customers can record up to 200MB per note

Check the Evernote website at www.evernote.com for current pricing for the above plans. The size of an audio recording will vary depending on the content of your recording and your device. And keep in mind that if your audio recording exceeds the total note size limit, your note will not sync to Evernote. It will only save on that device. In my experience 1 minute of recording time is a little less than 1MB. Again this can vary. I recommend creating some test recordings before recording an important interview so that you get a feel for how it works and the size of the files. To see the file size of a recording, download it to your computer using the procedure described previously. Locate the file on your hard drive, right-click on it, and click Properties. There you will find the audio file size.

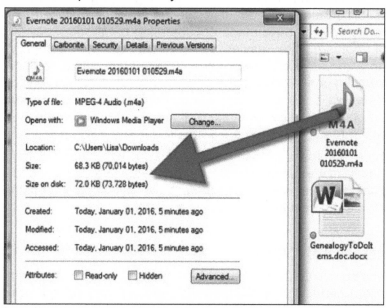

Based on my device's performance of approximately 3/4 of 1 MB (75 KB) per minute recorded, I err on the safe side and call it 1 minute per 1 MB. That way if I start to approach 50 minutes, I know it's time to stop and save. You can always start a new recording. And you can add typed notes to the audio recording note so you can add details about the order of the recordings in addition to other source information.

If you have a pre-recorded audio file from another program and you want to include it in Evernote, you can drag and drop the file right into Evernote to create a new note or drop it into an existing note. Again, keep in mind the file size at it does count toward your monthly upload limits. Review the Notetaking chapter for more on Evernote. You can also check out my quick reference guide *Evernote for Genealogists* for more details and tips on how to get started using Evernote on your computer. And we regularly cover Evernote on the Genealogy Gems blog. Here's the link to all of my past articles: http://lisalouisecooke.com/category/evernote-2/.

Chapter 8: Photos

Old family photos are some of the brightest gems along our research path. They deserve special attention and care. And mobile devices have made documenting our modern day lives via photos quicker, easier, and cheaper than ever before. We can also use our phone's camera to capture pages in books, microfilm projected onto the bed of a microfilm reader, plaques on the walls of historical buildings, tombstones in cemeteries, and countless other genealogical items. This all sounds great, but the result is that we are deluged with photos.

There are loads of apps that can work with your old family photos as well as the photos you're snapping today. My goal is to identify the various tasks we face with photos, and then provide the best apps for each job.

Capturing Photos

Let's start with taking photos. Your mobile device comes with a built-in camera. The features included will vary based on the platform (Apple, Android) and the device itself. Generally, the camera on your device will be able to take photos, videos and even panoramic photos.

Once you've captured an image, you can access it in Photos (iOS) and Gallery (Android), where you can apply basic editing and enhancements. Options include crop, add a filter, adjust light and color, etc. For more advanced editing features, I've got some apps for you in the *Working with Photos* section coming up later in this chapter.

As you pursue your family history, you will inevitably find yourself taking photos of other people's photos. If you are fortunate enough to have a relative share a beloved photo album with you, and you want to quickly and easily capture it, here are some reliable options.

Photomyne Pro – Album Scanner

By Photomyne LTD

Price: $4.99

Available: App Store

Google Play alternative: Album Scanner for memories

This app provides a convenient way to capture groups of photos. When enjoying a family member's photo album you may not have an opportunity to spend hours scanning each photo individually. And most folks aren't excited at the prospect of lending out their treasured albums. Photomyne allows you to quickly and easily scan multiple photos at one time. The app will automatically crop the photos it identifies, and let you easily adjust or mark missing ones.

Use the app to take pictures of your album pages or individual photos. The photos are automatically cropped and color corrected. Save the photos in albums, add dates and descriptions, and tag family and friends. Wrap it all up by saving the photos to your device. You can even share the images on Facebook and via email.

Storing and Organizing Photos

Photo storage and organization has been a problem ever since the camera was invented. I'll never forget being 6 years old and opening one of my Grandmother's closets to discover photos, loose and in boxes, piled high on her wedding cedar chest. Today, the challenge is even greater as photos pile up faster than ever now that capturing them digitally is so easy. Here are the basics on what you need to know about taming your digital images.

iCloud Photo Library

By Apple

Price: Free (with upgrade options)

Available: iOS version 8.3 and later

Photo management has evolved over the years on Apple devices. For many users, the changes have not necessarily made things easier, but rather caused more confusion. Let's clear that up so that you can get the most from your iPad's ability to take great photos. But as always, keep in mind that these current options and settings are subject to change, as Apple frequently releases updates.

As I mentioned at the beginning of this chapter, the photos you take can be found in the Photos app that comes on every Apple mobile device. In the Photos app, tap Albums, and you will find the Camera Roll album. This is where all of the photos and videos you have taken with that device are stored. They will stay there until you delete them. The photos are presented chronologically, starting with the most recent.

Over the life of your iPad or iPhone you can end up with more photos than you have storage. You may also have more than one Apple mobile device in your family, and you don't want the access to your photos to be restricted to the device with which they were taken. iCloud Photo Library is Apple's answer to these problems.

iCloud Photo Library is a Cloud service that works with the Photos app to keep your photos and videos stored in the cloud and up to date on your iPhone, iPad, iPod Touch, Mac, and iCloud.com. When activated, it automatically stores all of the photos and videos that you add from an iOS or Mac device in their original formats, including JPEG, RAW, PNG, GIF, TIFF, and MP4.You can also access your entire photo library from the Photos app on iCloud.com. This is invaluable if your device becomes lost, stolen, or damaged.

The benefit to using this service is that iCloud can help free up space on your iOS device. All of your full-resolution photos and videos are stored in iCloud in their original formats, while lower-resolution, storage-saving versions are kept on your iOS device. That way you can access more photos and videos on your device while taking up less space. Go to your Settings > iCloud > Photos to see if the photos on your phone are being kept in storage-saving mode or in full resolution. You'll see the options for Optimize iPhone Storage which is the storage-saving mode, or Download and Keep Originals, which is the full resolution.

Getting Started

To use iCloud Photo Library you need an Apple ID, a device with the most recent version of iOS (mobile) or OS X (Mac computer), and enough storage in your iCloud account to save your photos.

To turn on iCloud Photo Library in iOS 8.3 or later, go to Settings > iCloud > Photos, then turn on iCloud Photo Library.

When you turn on iCloud Photo Library on your iOS device or Mac, your photos and videos on that device will upload to iCloud. You must be connected to the Internet with Wi-Fi, and your battery must be charged.

When you access your Photos app, you will also notice that the Camera Roll is now called All Photos. The All Photos album shows you all of your photos and videos together, just like the Camera Roll, except it now includes the date and location they were taken.

As I mentioned earlier, the number of photos and videos you can store depends on your available iCloud storage. Currently, when you sign up for iCloud, you automatically get 5 GB of free storage. This storage space is also used to store all of your other data that is backed up to the iCloud such as your email, contacts, app data, etc. (Go to Settings > iCloud > Backup to turn this feature on or off.)

When it comes to backing up your photos and videos as well, 5 GB might not be enough for your purposes. You can see how much storage you have available under Settings > iCloud > Storage. Tap Manage Storage or visit iCloud.com to see how much of your storage it taken up by photos and backups. If you need more storage, several iCloud storage plans are available from 50 GB up to 1 TB *(for current limits and pricing visit https://support.apple.com/en-us/HT201238).*

Organization

In your Photos app, under the Photos icon (instead of Albums), iCloud Photo Library keeps your photos and videos organized chronologically into:

- Moments – groups the photos and videos that were taken around the same time and location
- Collections – broader groups of photos by location and a larger date range
- Years – all photos grouped by the year taken

You will notice that the thumbnail view of your photos gets smaller with each view setting. If you tap and hold your finger on the screen, you can move it across your photos to see a bigger pop-up view of each photo. Release your finger to select that photo for full-screen viewing.

Organize your photos further by marking your favorites or creating albums.

How to create an Album:

1. Tap the blue plus icon at the top of the screen
2. A pop-up window will appear asking for an album title
3. Enter a title using the on-screen keyboard
4. Tap the Save button
5. Next add images to the new album. A window will automatically appear containing all the available images on your device, organized by Moments.
6. Tap on as many images as you want
7. Tap the Done button
8. The selected images will be added to your new album

Keep in mind that even when you organize your photos into albums on your device, you must keep the original photo in your All Photos album. If you delete a photo from All Photos, it will be deleted from all albums that include it. If you delete a photo by mistake or need to retrieve it, you can access the Recently Deleted album. Photos and videos are stored here for 30 days before being permanently deleted, and the album will show you how many days are remaining before deletion for each one.

Siri (Apple's "intelligent assistant") can help you quickly search for a particular set of photos. (We will be talking a lot more about Siri later on in the *Fabulous Mobile Tips and Tricks* chapter) For example, say "Show me photos from my trip to Salt Lake City last February," and Siri will pull them up on your screen. If you do not want to record the location where you took the photo, go to Settings > Privacy > Location Services. You can turn Location Services completely off, or you can tap Camera from the list of apps and select Never.

Demystifying Photo Management

Have you ever noticed that when you delete a photo from one device it sometimes still appears on your other devices? When it comes to deleting photos, it is all about where you do the deleting.

When you take a photo with your iPhone or iPad it is automatically saved to that specific device's Camera Roll. The photo is also uploaded to the Photo Stream on all of your shared devices (via WiFi connection).

Photo Stream

Photo Stream stores your most recent 1000 photos or the last 30 days of images, whichever is greater. (It does not use your iCloud storage allotment.) This allows you to view and import your most recent photos to all of your devices. Photo Stream does not upload and sync videos.

Photos that you take with your Apple device will automatically upload to My Photo Stream when you leave the Camera app and connect to Wi-Fi. Photo Stream will share with devices that share the same iCloud account. So for example, if you and your spouse use the same iTunes/iCloud account, all the photos you both take with your phones will show up on both of your phones and iPads.

The Photo Stream automatically downloads reduced resolution versions of your photos which speeds downloads and saves storage space. Full-sized versions are stored in the iCloud Photo Library.

To access your Photo Stream in the Photos app, tap Albums (at the bottom of the screen), and then tap My Photo Stream.

Photo Stream is compatible across all of your devices that support iCloud including iPhone, iPad, Mac and PC. In order to use the Photo Stream you will need to make sure that the My Photo Stream button is turned on in Settings, under Photos & Camera. Alternatively you can go to Settings > iCloud > Photos, then turn on My Photo Stream. (Note: you also need a WiFi connection and at least 20% battery.) It is not necessary to turn on photo stream in both places in Settings.

It's important to think of My Photo Stream as a completely separate album from the Camera Roll which constantly updates to only include your most recent photos. For example, if you snapped a photo with your phone and you want a permanent copy saved to your iPad, you can view the photo in My Photo Stream and then select Save Image. This will save a copy to your iPad's Camera Roll that won't disappear as Photo Stream refreshes. Additionally, in order to completely delete a photo when My Photo Stream is enabled, the photo must be deleted from both the Camera Roll of the device that you used to take the photo, and from the My Photo Stream album. In some instances you may take a photo that you only want stored on the device that you took it with, and not on all of your devices. In that case, select and delete the photo from within the My Photo Stream album, which will delete the photo from your Photo Stream but retain the original copy in your device's Camera Roll.

Apple continues to refine its operating system and it is very possible that the current arrangement for photos will change. I wouldn't be surprised to see Photo Stream eliminated entirely at some point in the future. But for now, I hope this section has helped demystify how it currently works.

Shared

Shared is another feature in the Photos app that allows you to easily send photos and videos to other iCloud users. They can like and comment on your photos, as well as share their own photos with you. You can save photos that they have shared with you to your Camera Roll.

Google Photos

by Google, Inc.

Price: Free (upgrade options available)

Available: App Store, Google Play

Google Photos is not only available for both iOS and Android devices, but there is also an online version available for Mac and Windows PCs. Using the same Google Account that you use for Gmail, this is a convenient service to store all of your photos and videos from all of your devices in one place.

Getting Started

When you download and launch the Google Photos app, sign in to your Google account. It will ask for permission to access your photo library, select OK. Next you need to decide if you want to store your pictures in their full size, or in high quality. If you select high quality, your images will be compressed and you will have free unlimited storage. The quality is extremely good and the difference between the original and the compressed version is practically indistinguishable.

If you choose to upload your photos in their original size, you will be limited to 15GB of free storage. This storage is shared by all of your Google services such as Gmail, Google Docs, etc. You may purchase additional storage at www.google.com/settings/storage. The app provides a link to information about these options to help you decide, and you can always change your mind later in the Settings.

Google Photos only backs up your photos when you open the Google Photos app. It currently is not able to run in the background and upload whenever you take a picture. You can make a choice about whether you want Google Photos to automatically upload any new photos every time you open the app, or if you want to be selective about which items are backed up. To back up photos automatically, go to the settings in the Google Photos app. Tap Back up & sync and then tap again to turn on Back up & sync. If you want Google Photos to only back up the photos of your choosing:

1. Turn off Back up & sync in the settings

2. When you are on the home screen all the images that are on your device will be displayed

3. Tap the three dots in the top right corner

4. Tap Select

5. Tap each photo and video you want to back up to Google Photos

6. Tap the three dots again

7. Tap Back up

Uploading

Now your device will begin uploading your library of photos and videos to the Cloud. This can be time consuming if you have a lot of photos, so I suggest plugging into a power source and allowing it to back up overnight. One frustrating aspect of this process is that the uploading pauses if you do not have the Google Photos app open on your screen, so you can't multitask or turn your screen off without pausing the upload. To make sure this goes smoothly here are some steps to follow:

1. Go to the Settings app

2. Tap General

3. Tap Auto-Lock

4. Select Never

5. Return to the Google Photos app

6. Plug into a power source

7. Allow the app to stay open until the upload is complete

8. When finished, be sure to reset your Auto-Lock to the desired amount of time so you don't eat up your battery later

Organization

Google Photos automatically displays your photos and videos chronologically by the date taken, most recent photos being first. You can set the images to be shown by date, month, or year. As you scroll, a small button will appear on the right side of the screen that you can drag up and down to scroll more quickly.

As soon as your photos and videos start uploading, Google Photos starts going through your images and creating short videos, animations, collages, and more. This service is called Assistant. When you open the Google Photos app, swipe to the right to get to the Assistant screen. The Assistant will present "cards" offering you photo and video compilations. You can choose to add a compilation to your library, or you can discard it by swiping the card to the right. You can also make changes. For example, in a pre-created movie, you can change the music selection, filters, and remove any images you don't want included.

These fun creations might inspire you to make one of your own:

1. Tap the + sign at the top right of the screen

2. The Create New screen will open

3. Choose if you would like to create a new album, movie, story, animation, or collage

4. Select the photos you want to include

5. Tap Create

6. Be sure to save when you are done editing by tapping the three dots at the top right of the editing screen and selecting Download. This will to add it to your Camera Roll or Add to Album to just save to Google Photos

Search

One of the best features of Google Photos is Search. It's terrific because it retrieves photos by analyzing the content of the photos and the date and time it was taken.

Tap the magnifying glass at the bottom left of the Home screen and you are presented with pictures automatically grouped by category:

- *People* - Google recognizes faces in each image and groups them together

- *Places* - groups by the location where the images were taken

- *Things* - groups images by topics such as Halloween, cars, and selfies

You can use the search box at the top to search for almost anything. For example, I can search for "conference" and Google will find all of the photos that look like they were taken at a genealogy conference.

All of your photos, videos, albums and creations in Google Photos can be shared right from the app with all the usual services like Facebook, Twitter, email, etc.

Working with Photos

We aren't done yet. Capturing photos is just the beginning. Here are my favorite apps for creatively working with and sharing photos and other images:

Adobe Photoshop Express

by Adobe Systems Incorporated

Price: Free

Available: App Store and Google Play

Adobe is the leading name in photo editing and the Adobe Photoshop Express app gives you the ability to simply and quickly edit and share your photos. It's also been improved since I last discussed it in my book, *Turn Your iPad into a Genealogy Powerhouse.*

With Adobe Photoshop Express you can:

- Crop, straighten, rotate, and flip your photos
- Adjust exposure, brightness and contrast, color, and balance
- Convert to black & white, colorize, sketch, soft focus, sharpen, reduce noise
- Purchase additional effects and borders

And the good news is that now you can access your photos straight from Dropbox (as well as Adobe Creative Cloud, Revel, and Facebook).

Photo Restoration

If you want to restore old family photos, this app is now also capable of doing a lovely job with the new Blemish Removal tool.

I recommend copying the old photos that you want to edit to a dedicated folder on Dropbox. Leave your master digital copies where they are on your computer.

How to add photos to Adobe Photoshop Express:

1. On the computer where your photos are stored, go into Dropbox (either your Dropbox desktop application, or sign in to your account at www.dropbox.com.)
2. Create a folder called "Photos for Editing"
3. Save copies of the photos you want to edit into the folder you created, leaving the originals where they are on your hard drive.
4. On your tablet, tap the Adobe Photoshop Express app.
5. Tap Dropbox. (See the chapter on File Sharing and Storage for more information on Dropbox.)
6. Tap the "Photos for Editing" folder
7. Tap the photo you want to edit.

8. The photo is now on your screen and ready to edit and embellish.

9. When editing is complete, tap Close, then Save.

Here is a photo of my great grandfather. On the left is the original scan, and on the right I have done just a few minutes of restoration with the Blemish Removal tool (the icon looks like a Band-Aid). After the touch up I applied the Dream filter which provided a bit more clarity and softened the rough spots in the background. Dream is one of the many free "Looks" available in the app, in addition to "Premium Looks" filters that you can purchase. And I love the fact that if I find a certain combination of filters is working well for me, I can save it under "My Looks." This saves me time in the future because with one tap I can apply my special mix.

Color Splash for iPad

by Pocket Pixels, Inc.

Price: $1.99

Available: App Store

If you really want to bring focus to a particular area of a photo, or you just want to have some fun, there's an app for that: ColorSplash!

The premise is simple: the app converts your photo to black and white, and then when in Color mode you use your finger as a brush to "paint" desired areas of your image back to the original color. The color brings fun and 'pop' to what you want the focal point to be. And in Gray mode you can always paint regions back to black and white.

Zoom in and out using the pinch gesture to work on the fine details of your picture. You can also move around the image using two fingers

You can take a photo right from within the app, or grab your photos from other locations such as your camera roll Facebook, Instagram, Flickr, Picasa, and Dropbox.

Below is an example of some fun I had. (I realize this example will be in black and white in the print version of this book, but trust me, it's a cool effect. Those of you reading the digital ebook will see it in color.) The photo on the far left is the original color photo. The photo in middle has been converted to black and white with only my grandmother's floral dress returned to color in Color Splash. The photo on the right has become a shared memory using Retype. It says *"Favorite Memories: Grandma's Flowered Dresses."* And Retype is coming up next!

Android Alternative to Color Splash for iPad: Color Splash FX

by androidslide

Price: Free

Available: Play Store

Retype

by Sumoing Ltd

Price: $2.99

Available: App Store

This is the one app that I hesitated to put in this book. Not because I wasn't sure it was worth your time. Rather, it was all selfish on my part! I use Retype to create spectacularly fun and interesting images for my Genealogy Gems website. It's my visual ace in the hole and I sort of hate to make it widely known. But I love my readers, so it's not an option, I have to tell you about it!

Retype adds stylish graphic text to images. Doesn't exactly sound earth shattering, does it? But images you create with this app have the ability to really shake up your relatives and your family tree.

Mobile is a hot trend, and awesome images are even hotter. If you want to avoid glazed over looks from your non-genealogist relatives (particularly kids and grandkids) then you've got to start dishing up the family history in riveting ways. An image created with Retype will captivate them, and dare I say it, actually motivate them to share the image with their family and friends. Think of it as a Mad Men PR campaign and you're the top exec! Let me share one of the images I made recently and then I'll walk you through how to create your own.

Here's one of my favorite photos of my uncle Buzz when he was a kid (center).

I added a simple caption that takes the pic from cute to captivating.

Sharing a photo like this on Facebook or Instagram can start all kinds of family conversation. I could upload this to Facebook and ask the questions like: "Who remembers when this was taken?" Or comment "Thankfully, I don't think he's changed much - still a bundle of joy!" Comments are guaranteed to flow and your family will start to associate fun with family history and looking back through the years. You might even get lucky and hear some new stories!

How to use Retype to create images:

Open the Retype app and you'll be greeted by a colorful image with some catchy text like "What You Do Today Can Improve All Your Tomorrows" (that's certainly what I'm striving to accomplish with this book.) Retype is loaded with great images and tons of pithy sayings to help you quickly create an image that captures your mood.

Tap the text on the image and your keyboard will appear and the text will be ready for you to edit. If this saying doesn't capture your fancy, tap the three horizontal line icon in the upper left corner to peruse a myriad of sayings (which you can also create in a few other languages like Dutch and French.) For now, tap the check mark in the upper right corner to return to the home screen.

I like to start with the image and then select the text to suit. Tap the image icon to select a photo from the Retype gallery or select an image from your Camera Roll. If you have an image you want to use that you didn't snap with your device, just save it to an app like Dropbox or Google Drive and open it on your device. Take a screen shot (see *Functionality Tips and Tricks* for how to do this) and edit as desired (it may need some cropping). Now you have the image in your photo roll ready to use in Retype.

Tap the desired image and it will appear on the Retype home screen. Now you're ready to add text. Again, you can make it your own by editing the existing text, or select from the text options.

FAVORITE MEMORIES: GRANDMA'S FLOWERED DRESSES

Now the real fun begins! It's time to add some real flair to your text. You'll notice that the text is already in a pretty snazzy font, but there are loads of fonts to choose from. At the bottom of the screen you'll see fonts such as Vintage, The Queen, Newspaper, Loose Brushwork, and more. Slide the list of fonts to reveal all the options. I used Core Circus for Buzz's image. Select a font and each time you tap it, your text will appear in a different version of the font. The variations are seemingly endless, and are a ton of fun to peruse. I can almost guarantee you will find a font and style that suits the mood you are trying to create. And I think that's what Retype is really all about: creating mood, and conveying emotion and story. It's a fabulous example of the fact that sometimes less is definitely more!

Once you've selected your font and style, it's time to select another terrific mood creator: color. Tap the circle icon that looks like an open camera lens and swipe through the color options. You'll quickly get a feel for what works with the image you have selected. I say *image* because I use Retype for so much more than just photos. It can even bring genealogical documents to life for non-genealogists. Imagine that!

Now it's time to consider dressing up the image itself. Tap the 'closed lens' icon to discover filter options. I don't tend to use these that much, but filters can occasionally add dramatic flair, or help an image step to the background a bit while the text shines.

There's also a Fade – Blur – Opacity option. Tap the three horizontal lines with dots icon and move the slider to the desired effect.

Not quite sure now about that font and style you selected? Simply tap the "T" icon to return to fonts.

When everything has come together just the way you like it, then it's time to save your image. From the home screen (not in text editing mode) tap the checkmark icon and you can then save the image to your photo roll, share it to Instagram, or open it in a number of apps such as Evernote, Facebook or Email. Tap "More" to see all your options and to turn on access to the desired app.

At first glance Retype may not look like an app for a genealogist, but in my book (and in this book!) it is an exciting and easy way to generate buzz, particularly through social media, with the next generation of genealogists and non-genealogists in my family. And that is extremely important, because they are ultimately the ones who will decide what becomes of all that we have lovingly assembled on our family.

Pocketbooth

By Project Box

Price: $1.99

Available: App Store, Google Play

Pocketbooth offers old-timey fun for the living, and a wonderful way to capture new memories!

This retro styled app provides loads of fun at family events. And my grandson loves to sit on my lap and take photos together just like in the old days when you would climb in a photo booth at the fair.

What's New: Pocketbooth has been updated to support the new retina display of the New iPad. The developers have also added printing and ordering options. And if you tap the shopping cart button for options to purchase effects "packs" for even more fun.

While this is my personal favorite app of this type, you'll find lots of options in both the App Store and Google Play by typing "photo booth" in the search box.

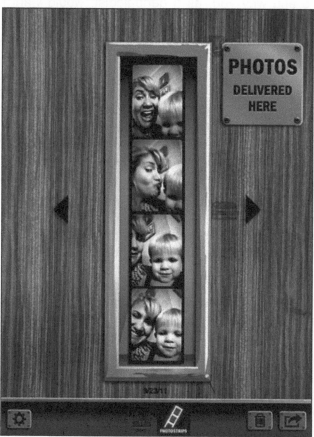

Chapter 9: Reading

There are two distinct types of digital reading we do as genealogists: web content and ebooks. I will address each and provide you with my favorite apps that make reading on your tablet not only convenient, but truly enjoyable.

Reading Content from the Web

As I travel and speak to genealogy groups, I like to ask how many people read genealogy blogs. I'm still surprised how few hands go up. Blogs are a resource still fairly untapped by the average family historian. So let's first discuss exactly what they are and why you, as a genealogist, would want to read them.

Blogs are websites, or are part of larger websites. For example, Ancestry's blog in part of the much larger Ancestry.com website. Like a column in a newspaper, they are typically written by one author, but in this case the articles are posted online rather than in print. The articles will appear in chronological order, with the most recent article at the top of the web page. Blogs are a convenient and easy way to publish information, and make it instantly available to the world.

The beauty of following and reading blogs in a *blog reader* like the ones I will be presenting in this chapter, is that you get to pick and choose which writers and subjects you receive. Instead of getting a newspaper with dozens of pages of content that don't interest you, you get to be the editor, compiling exactly what you want to read. In this chapter I will show you how to use blog reader apps to subscribe to the genealogy blogs that interest you, and have them delivered to your tablet or phone for free! No more going to the curb in your slippers to get the paper. It's all at your fingertips.

So who writes all of these blogs that I'm suggesting you will want to read? Librarians, archivists, researchers, storytellers, and genealogy businesses are all using blogs to communicate with their audiences. For example, if you want to be the first to sign up for the latest genealogy class at your local library, your best bet is to follow the library's blog, because that is likely where they will announce it. My own *Genealogy Gems* blog sprang up as a way for me to deliver genealogy news and information quickly, easily, and even creatively. Follow my blog with this RSS feed: http://www.genealogygems.com/rss.

The important take away here is that blogs are the way to stay up to date in the ever changing genealogy research landscape. I have selected two great blog reader apps to get you started that will put you in the editor's chair, *and* in-the-know.

Flipboard

by Flipboard, Inc.

Price: Free

Available: App Store, Google Play

When the iPad hit the market, it inspired a new generation of visually-oriented apps. One such app is Flipboard.

Flipboard takes full advantage of both the vibrant tablet display and finger-swiping functionality when delivering web content. It turns average blog posts, YouTube videos, and social media communications into a digital magazine-style format.

There are two distinct ways you can use Flipboard:

As a Blog Reader – you select and add the web content providers you want to follow to Flipboard. You can also read and follow other people's Flipboard magazines. Think of it like paper magazine subscriptions. Isn't it easier to subscribe to your favorite genealogy magazine and have it delivered to your mailbox at home rather than having to go to the store several times a month checking for the latest issue? That's the principle behind Flipboard. Your favorite blogs, video channels, and podcasts are delivered to your Flipboard app as soon as they are published. And best of all, for free!

As a Digital Magazine Creator – You won't actually be creating a magazine that you will sell on a magazine stand or on Amazon. A Flipboard "Magazine" is made up of your favorite blog articles, videos, podcast episodes etc. As you surf the web you can "flip" (save) **individual items** into the magazine that you create. It's much like pinning (saving) web items on

Pinterest. (We'll talk more about Pinterest in the upcoming Captivating Non-Genealogists chapter.)

Typically you would pick a theme for your magazine. For example, my first magazine was "Historic Newspapers." Whenever I found great content online about historic newspaper research, I saved it to my magazine. This is really helpful when you don't have time to read something, or you want to refer to the information in your future genealogical research. It's simply a collection of content you saved in an enjoyable magazine format. It reminders me of how my mom used to clip recipes and favorite articles out of newspapers and magazines. But rather than ending up with a drawer full of faded, disorganized clippings, you will have a beautiful and organized digital magazine. And magazines are easy to share, too.

Magazines are unique on Flipboard because they are stagnant. They are not tied to RSS feeds, so content is not automatically updating over time. It only updates when the owner of the magazine updates it or adds to it.

Using Flipboard as a Blog Reader

Now that I've made my best case for Flipboard, let's go back to the beginning and learn how to use it as a blog reader.

How to get started with Flipboard:

1. Download the app

2. Sign up, and sign in, with a free account

3. Tap the red ribbon in the upper right corner to go to your account dashboard

4. You'll see suggested topics listed under "Discover More" (and no, you won't see "genealogy" listed there). This is a good place to get some practice though. Tap a few topics that interest you, and tap the Follow button for a blog or two.

5. When you're done exploring the suggested topics, swipe the dashboard away to the right, or just tap on the homepage in the back ground.

6. Back on the home page, you will see a search box at the top. Here's where you can start digging deeper. Type keywords like "genealogy" or a blog title in the

search box. You'll immediately start to see other people's public free magazines on that topic listed, as well as other user profiles, and social networking results. You can follow other people who are on Twitter, Google+, YouTube, SoundCloud, Flickr, and Tumblr in Flipboard. Flipboard will suggest other people based on the word(s) you searched.

7. Results will automatically fill the page. You'll notice that Flipboard takes the incoming content and arranges it so it looks like a page in a magazine. You are seeing "snippets" or highlights of what each article or video is about, and usually an image from that item.

8. Swipe with our finger as if you were flipping pages in a book to see more from that person or blog.

9. Tap an item that looks interesting, and it will pop out of the page and fill the screen. When you're done with it, tap the back arrow and it will return to its spot on the page.

10. If you want to "follow" the blog (i.e. add the blog to your list of selected blogs so that you receive automatic updates), tap the Follow button at the top of the page. From that point forward it will appear on your dashboard for future reference. Blogs are published via RSS feeds, and that just means that articles will be instantly updated in Flipboard for you as the blogger publishes them. You never have to go checking a favorite site to see if there's anything new.

Using Flipboard as a Magazine Creator

I love creating magazines of my favorite web-based items. Here's a short list of some of the magazines I've created with Flipboard, which you are welcome to "follow" and enjoy:

- Using Newspapers for Genealogy and Family History at www.tinyurl.com/gennewspapers

- Using Historic Maps for Genealogy and Family History at www.tinyurl.com/genmaps

- RootsTech at www.Tinyurl.com/rootstech2014

- Genealogy Gems at http://tinyurl.com/gemsmag

- Mason Jar Mania (Yes, I'm obsessed with mason jars!) at http://tinyurl.com/masonmania

Or you can simply follow me (which includes all of my magazines) at https://flipboard.com/@gengems. As you create magazine, you can share them with others, and they can "follow" you too.

How to create a magazine in Flipboard:

1. Search for a keyword, phrase, title or person in the search box

2. Tap a result that looks interesting to you

3. When you find an article you want to "flip" into a magazine, tap the plus sign at the bottom of the page

4. In the pop up window tap Add to create a new magazine or tap an existing magazine that you want to add it to

You can also add web content to your Flipboard magazines from your web browser with Flipboard's free bookmarklet. Go to https://share.flipboard.com/p/mobilebookmarklet and follow the instructions for installing the bookmarklet button on your web browser, both on your tablet and your computer. This will allow you to add articles, videos, podcast episodes, etc. to your magazines from any web page.

To view your magazines, go back to the main screen and tap the red ribbon in the upper right corner. This will take you to your account dashboard and you will see all of your magazines displayed there. You'll also find other useful information including the Settings button (the gear icon). Settings is the place where you can change the font size to suit your needs and customize your Flipboard experience.

In 2014 I visited the Flipboard offices in Palo Alto, CA and interviewed Tom Lapin from their editorial team. You can listen to part one of that interview in Genealogy Gems Podcast Episode 186 and part two in Genealogy Gems Premium Podcast episode 106 *(access requires Premium membership)*.

Todd Lapin and me at the Flipboard offices, Palo Alto, CA

Feedly

by DevHD

Price: Free

Available: App Store, Google Play

Run a search on "genealogy" at the Blog Search Engine website at www.blogsearchengine.org and you'll receive well over 5,000,000 results. Talk about information overload! But there is a lot of great up-to-the-minute content out there on blogs that can assist your research and nurture your ongoing genealogical education.

Feedly offers an easy way to consume the specific online content you want, like genealogy blog articles and videos. It is a free online "content aggregator." That's just a techie way of saying it pulls together in one convenient location (the Feedly app) the most current information that appears on the websites you enjoy. No more having to remember and type your favorite websites addresses. No more searching through your web browser's bookmarks for links to websites. It's all in one place and it's the most recent content.

And when those providers publish new content (blog, podcast, video) on the web, it is automatically sent to your Feedly account. That way, you don't have to go in search of what's new. Instead, the latest content automatically comes to you.

Feedly works on web browsers on your computer, and mobile devices (Android & iOS). Its strength is how easy it makes adding and organizing web content. There are a few ways to add items to Feedly.

How to add content - Method #1:

1. In the search box, search for keywords and / or websites

2. Tap a selection from the results

3. Tap the green +feedly button

How to add content - Method #2:

When you identify a website that you want to add to Feedly, look for an orange RSS button on the site. If you find one, click it and see if the site offers an "add to Feedly" button.

If it doesn't have an Add to Feedly button, then that page is the RSS feed page. The RSS feed URL is the address that will allow you to subscribe to a website.

Copy the URL and paste it into Feedly's search box.

In addition to following blogs, you can also add your favorite genealogy-themed YouTube channels to Feedly.

How to add a YouTube channel to Feedly:

1. Copy the channel's home page URL address
2. Paste it into the Feedly search box
3. Add */feed* to the end of the address
4. Press Enter on your keyboard

Organize your feeds into categories such as:

- Libraries
- Archives
- Research locations
- Surnames
- Priority (include your list of "must read" items here!)

You can also choose how your feeds will be displayed: by title, magazine, or cards. This allows for quick scanning of post titles and usually includes a "snippet" view of the first few words, making it possible to very quickly decide which items to spend your time reading.

Whether you choose Feedly or Flipboard (or both) your online content consumption will be far more efficient and enjoyable.

Reading eBooks and Documents

Genealogists love books! We love to buy them, read them, and write in their margins. Even though we love paper, there are some pretty compelling reasons for making the move to ebooks.

The first reason (and one that others in your household will likely agree with whole-heartedly) is that book shelf "real estate" is always at a premium in the genealogist's home and office. Unfortunately there is a limit to space even though there is seemingly no limit to our thirst for books. Unlimited numbers of digital books can be collected and stored in the Cloud and accessed on your tablet and smartphone. Personally, I've really enjoyed reclaiming some family history display space that was once taken up completely by print books.

Second, you can take all those books with you by tossing your phone in your pocket. No more lugging book bags on research trips that threaten to dislocate your shoulder!

And third, ebooks are searchable. This feature is often overlooked and underutilized, but it is truly the genealogist's best friend. In a split second your eReader's search box can find any word or phrase you desire.

Free ebooks abound at websites like Google Books, and many libraries even loan ebooks. And of course you can now purchase them anytime, anywhere through iTunes, Google Play, and Amazon, just to name a few online stores.

Now that I've made the case for ebooks, let me tell you about some of the best eReaders available.

GoodReader

by Good.iWare Ltd.

Price: $4.99

Available: App Store

Several years ago I recommended GoodReader because it offered the ability to annotate PDF ebooks, a feature important to genealogists. Though it was robust then, it has not stagnated by any stretch of the imagination. It's been called "a Swiss army knife" and that is exactly what it is for readers and researchers.

GoodReader is first and foremost a top-notch tool for viewing and managing PDF documents. It is ideal for the genealogist since there are thousands (if not millions) of free historical books available in PDF form on Google Books alone. PDFs are also a common file format for research documents. You can do much more than just read PDFs though. If you like making notes in text and scribbling in the margins, you will love the extensive annotation tools. You can even edit and sign PDF documents using the versatile app.

Good Reader can open even the largest PDF files. Once opened you can crop pages, insert, delete, rotate and rearrange pages, split and merge PDFs, and even extract and email individual pages from a large PDF.

GoodReader has expanded its eReader functionality to include all types of media that you may want to use. With the latest version you can:

- View MS Office, TXT, HTML documents
- View pictures

- listen to audio
- watch video

GoodReader makes an easy job of maintaining your collection of files and folders no matter how large. You can stay organized by copying, moving, renaming and compressing your files and folders. And you can also automatically synchronize your folders to remote server computers for storage, or use WiFi or USB to exchange files with your computer.

One of the newest features is that GoodReader now works with Bluetooth foot pedal page turners. That was a head-scratcher for me the first time I read it. But this could be a very handy feature when you want to read hands-free. A quick search of Amazon revealed several foot pedals on the market. They are geared towards musicians who want to be able to turn the page of music on their iPad without using their hands. A press of the foot pedal turns the page. I'm sure some creative genealogists out there wouldn't mind having hands free to perform tasks while still devouring their favorite tomes.

GoodReader has a straight-forward online user manual available at http://www.goodreader.com/gr-man.html.

Play Books

by Google, Inc.

Price: Free

Available: App Store, included on Android

I've written and lectured on the immense genealogical value of Google Books for years. In fact you'll find an entire chapter dedicated to it in my book *The Genealogist's Google Toolbox, Second Edition.* If using Google Books for genealogy is new to you, I highly recommend that you read up on it and start using it. You'll be glad you did!

It's rather easy to confuse Google Play Books and Google Books. For Google, dealing with books has definitely been a work in progress. Long-time Google Books users will remember when www.books.google.com was the only URL for Google Books. Then one day the page suddenly sported two searches boxes: one for Google Books and one for books at the Google Play Store.

As of this writing the URL looks more like the basic Google search page, with just the slight variation of the word "Books" appearing below the logo, and the addition of "My library". The single sentence that appears on the page helps explain the difference. "Search the world's most comprehensive index of full-text books." This is clearly not the same as the Play Store where you can shop a huge selection of books, as well as take advantage of a select number of free ebooks. However, the phrase "My library" found on this page is the signal that there is a distinct relationship between the two. Understanding that connection will help you get the full value from the Play Books app.

Play Books is:

- an excellent ebook reader

- an extensive ebook Store

- a powerful tool for accessing your MyLibrary. MyLibrary is where you can manage your ebooks from both Google Books and the Google Play Store.

Getting Started

If you have an Android tablet, you will likely already find the Play Books app on your home screen. iPad users can download the app for free in the App Store. Sign in with your free Google account. You already have a free Google account if you use Gmail. If you have already used Google Books with that account (perhaps on another device such as your home computer) the books that you downloaded will appear in MyLibrary. You will also see any books that you purchased under that account at the Play Store.

App Features

There are loads of reasons to love Play Books:

- Your library of ebooks stays current thanks to synchronization when connected to the internet.

- Because of synchronization, the position on the page where you stop reading is saved and synced. This means you can pick up reading where you left off on any of your computing devices.

- You have the flexibility to download your ebooks for offline reading, or access them from Google's servers with an internet connection, saving your device's storage space.

- You can customize your reading experience by changing fonts, line height, brightness, and using night-reading mode.

- As a researcher, you'll love being able to search within any book for specific text. You can also bookmark key pages, highlight relevant text, and add research notes. And again, thanks to the Cloud, all of your research annotations will synchronize across your various devices.

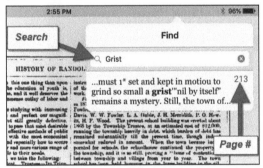

- When you encounter an unfamiliar word, press and hold the word to highlight it, and receive the definition.

- You can get more help when you need it. For example, tap on the name of a location in a text to pull up an information card about that place, as well as access to more information on Wikipedia or Google.

- When you're on the go and aren't free to read, you can continue your research by listening to your books (when allowed by the publisher) with the text-to-speech feature. On Android go to Menu > Settings > Automatically Read Aloud. (iOS: text-to-speech isn't built into Play Books, but you can turn on "VoiceOver" by going to your device's Settings > General > Accessibility > VoiceOver > On.)

- Language doesn't have to be a barrier to international genealogical research because the app can translate text.

One of the features that I think is essential to an eReader is the ability to upload your own ebooks. Play Books allows you to upload ePUB or PDF books to your personal MyLibrary.

How to upload ebooks and PDFs to Play Books on Android:

1. Open Play Books

2. Tap Menu > Settings > Enable PDF uploading

3. Exit the app

4. Download a PDF or ePUB file on your device and touch Upload to Play Books

How to upload ebooks and PDFs to Play Books on iOS:

1. There's no need for iPad or iPhone users to "enable PDF uploading" in the app. You can go straight to Safari to access an ebook online. In my case, I keep a folder called "ebooks" in Dropbox (covered in the *File Storage & Management* chapter) that contains ebooks that I've collected from a variety of sources.

2. Tap the file in Dropbox

3. Tap Share

4. Tap Copy to Play Books

While Play Books doesn't support uploading file types other than ePUB and PDF, it is pretty easy to convert the rare books you find that aren't in one of these two formats. There are several websites that can do this for you. Calibre (at http://calibre-ebook.com) is one of the most popular.

Limitations

In addition to the file type limitation, there are a few other limitations to be aware of with Play Books:

- You can't upload ebooks with DRM (which stands for digital rights management. These files restrict the usage of proprietary software, hardware, or content.)

- The file uploaded must be smaller than 100MB in size.

- You can upload up to1,000 files.

Overall, Play Books is a powerhouse of an eReader!

iBooks

by Apple

Price: Free

Available: App Store

The iPad comes with its own book reader called iBooks. You can purchase books through the iBooks Store in the app, and then organize and read them in iBooks. The app is graphically pleasing with its beautiful and easy-to-browse bookshelf. Just tap a book to open it, flip through pages with a swipe of the finger, and bookmark or add notes to key passages.

Currently, iBooks does not allow you to annotate PDF documents (GoodReader is the best choice for that), but you can make notes and highlight ebooks. Press and hold a word on the page you are viewing, and then select the desired amount of text you want to include in the note or highlight. Tap Note, and a small box will appear for you to type your notes. When finished, tap anywhere on the page to close the note. The text you selected will now be highlighted, and you can select the highlight color if you want to color-code. You can access the note by tapping the highlighted text. To access all of the notes you have made in that book, tap the menu icon in the top left corner.

iBooks also takes advantage of iCloud. By backing up your books to iCloud, you can access them across multiple devices that are signed into the same account. It even saves where you left off, and allows you to pick up at the same spot on a different device.

Your iPhone or iPad will adjust the brightness automatically when reading in dim light. iBooks will also alert you if a book you've purchased has a newly updated edition available. You can download the updated version for free, and it will replace the old version in your library.

iBooks supports the ePUB file format, PDFs, MP3 audiobooks, AAC audiobooks, and audiobooks from www.audible.com. If you want to add books, audiobooks, and PDFs from outside the iBooks Store or audible.com, they need to be DRM-free. Some PDFs might not be compatible with iBooks. Books from sources like Kindle, Nook, and Google Books use their own DRM and some cases their own file formats, which often prevents them from being transferred to iBooks.

Compatible, DRM-free eBooks that you obtain through other online sources can be added to iBooks.

How to open a PDF/ePUB file in Safari and save it to iBooks:

1. Open the PDF document in Safari on your iPad

2. Tap on the document

3. Tap the "Open in iBooks" button that appears in the upper right corner

4. The PDF will be added to your iBooks collection in your iPad

How to open a PDF/ePUB file in Dropbox and save it to iBooks:

1. Open the ebook in the Dropbox app

2. Tap the Share button in the top right corner

4. Tap "Open in…"

5. A text box will appear that says Exporting. Wait for it to finish.

6. Tap Copy to iBooks

7. iBooks will open and your ebook will now appear on your iBookshelf

Chapter 10:
Collaboration & Communication

One of the areas where emerging technology has been the biggest boon for genealogists has been *connection*. Connecting with long lost cousins and collaborating with researchers who live miles away has never been easier or less expensive. Whether you post, Skype or just want to obtain a fresh set of eyes on a genealogical research challenge, these apps will help you do it faster, easier, and on the go.

Facebook

by Facebook, Inc.

Price: Free

Available: App Store, Google Play

Facebook, which is dominating the social media space, has become a mecca for genealogists to make connections. There are a number of ways that genealogists use Facebook for their family history:

- Connect with unknown living relatives
- Connect with known relatives
- Connect with like-minded genealogists on shared topics of interest
- Connect with genealogists to obtain assistance
- Connect with groups that have historical information that adds value to your family history

If you do not currently use Facebook or would like a more in-depth tutorial on how to use it for genealogy, check out www.GenealogyGems.com/?s=facebook. You'll find great articles that show you how to use Facebook for the tasks above. But in this section, we will focus primarily on the differences between the desktop version of Facebook, and the app version for mobile devices.

So why should you download the Facebook app on your tablet when you can just open up the web browser and go to Facebook.com? That's a good question. The answer is that the app is more compatible with smaller devices. Photos and text will appear much bigger and fit to the smaller screen, versus having to zoom in, or swipe back and forth in order to see everything on the page. It's also easier to tap on icons and links. Smaller screens mean limited space, so the app focuses on making the primary features prominent and removing clutter for a faster, simplified experience.

And with all this genealogical connecting in mind, the Facebook app has a lot to offer. While it is not as full featured as its desktop counterpart, it does give you a collection of the most popular features including:

- Share high-resolution photos and view others' photos in album format
- Navigate quickly by tapping, sliding, or pinching to move from one screen to another
- Access your favorite Facebook apps and games
- Stream your News Feed
- Post comments and questions
- See who is nearby geographically
- Plan an event and stay in contact with those attending

After you download the app and tap to open it, enter your email or phone number and your password (or sign up for Facebook). This will keep you signed in to Facebook whenever you use the app. But if you share your device, you also have the option to save multiple user accounts, and add 4-digit passcodes instead of typing in full usernames and passwords.

Like most people, I originally signed up for Facebook on my desktop computer, and set it up to email me the most important posts and notifications. But when I opened my email on my phone, and tapped the link to the Facebook post, it would take me to the Facebook app and prompt me to sign in. I already had the Facebook app downloaded and signed in, so I wasn't sure why tapping links required me to sign in, when tapping the app did not. Thankfully, it turned out there was a simple solution.

On your mobile device, go to Settings > Facebook, and sign in with your email and password. This will keep your mobile device signed in to your Facebook account at all times. That way, when you click a link to Facebook from your email, your web browser, or any app other than the Facebook app, you will be automatically signed in. You can also adjust some privacy settings here, such as your contacts, calendars, location, and notifications.

With the Facebook app, at the top of your home page, you will see the same search bar and link to your profile page that you see on the desktop version. The other icons that you are used to seeing have been moved to the bottom of the app such as:

News Feed – Your home page when you sign in, to see your friends' posts. A little trick: if you've been scrolling down your newsfeed for a while and want to get back to the top, tap the News Feed icon and you will be taken instantly back to the most recent post.

Requests – Shows you any new friend requests, as well as people you may know with the option to add them as a friend or remove them from the list.

Messenger – This is Facebook's instant messaging service. You will need to download their Messenger app if you want to use this feature.

Notifications – Here you will see where your friends have liked or commented on your posts, tagged you in a post or photo, or invited you to an event. You can customize your notifications in the app's settings.

More – This is where you can see your friends list, events, groups, apps, and settings.

You may also notice that holding your tablet vertical or horizontal changes what you see. When holding your tablet vertical, you will just see your news feed and options at the top and bottom of the app. But if you hold your tablet horizontal, you will see more of the features that you would see on the desktop version, such as the chat box (showing which of your friends are online available to chat), what topics are trending in discussions/shares, apps or games, and recently active groups. What you see here may vary, depending on your Facebook activity and which friends you interact with the most on Facebook.

The app version of Facebook is simpler, cleaner, and focuses mainly on the news feed. You can still access everything you would on the desktop version, tucked away so that it doesn't clutter up your viewing when you're on the go.

Skype

by Skype Communications S.a.rl.

Price: Free

Available: App Store, Google Play

When I hit the road to speak to genealogy audiences I rely heavily on my Skype app to keep me connected. I can call anyone I need to get in touch with just like I do on my home computer. And a video chat with my grandson in the evening is the perfect way to end the day.

This app takes advantage of your tablet's full screen video. Call, video chat, or instant message anyone with a Skype account for free. Plus, you can purchase Skype Credit to call landlines and mobile phones at really low rates nationally and internationally.

FaceTime

by Apple

Price: Free

Available: App Store (included on your iPad)

Make video calls for free over WiFi or a cellular network from your iPhone, iPad, iPod Touch or Mac to someone else's Apple device. You can choose in the Settings which email addresses and phone numbers you want people to use to contact you for FaceTime calls. In Settings > FaceTime you can choose which email address or phone number you want to appear during outgoing FaceTime calls as well.

To start a video call with someone in the FaceTime app, type the name of a person in the search box at the top. If the contact has a compatible Apple device that allows for FaceTime, it will say FaceTime and you can tap the video camera icon or call icon.

Remember your iPhone and iPad have two built in cameras, the one facing you and one on the back. While you are on a FaceTime call you can easily switch back and forth between the two by tapping the button with the arrows going in a circle.

Google Translate

by Google

Price: Free

Available: App Store, Google Play

Google Translate is one of the most exciting apps in recent years. It strives to remove language barriers, both text and spoken.

The Google Translate app can:

- translate text (90 languages)
- use your camera to translate text (26 languages)
- support two-way automatic speech translation (40 languages)

It therefore offers a wide range of opportunities for overcoming language barriers in your genealogy research. Examples include:

- plaques on historic buildings
- road signs while traveling
- books and documents

Conversation Translation

If you are headed to an archive in another country, Google Translate can help you converse with others who speak a different language.

How to translate a conversation:

1. Select the applicable languages
2. Tap the microphone button
3. Speak into the device
4. Hear the translation
5. Touch the mic to listen for both languages

Speak either language to have a conversation

Saving Translations

When conducting research in foreign language records such as church records, it is not uncommon to turn to certain words and phrases repeatedly. With Google Translate you can ask for the translation once and then save it by tapping the star icon on the translation. This saves it to your Phrasebook, which you will find when you tap the menu (3 vertical dots). Tap the Phrasebook's Sync button to keep your common phrases synced across all of your devices. Over time you can build a handy genealogical collection.

Also in the menu you will find Settings. Here you can select dialects, and see the available languages for the various tools.

Instant Camera Translation

One of the incredible strengths of the Google Translate app is that it harnesses your device's camera, mixes it with a bit of Optical Character Recognition (OCR) and serves up translations in real time. Some of the original proposed uses of this technology were to use your camera to walk up to a street sign in a foreign country, hold your camera up to it, and Google Translate would display the sign translated into your native language. Pretty amazing! I couldn't help, however, bridging from there to more pressing needs I have as a genealogist. For instance, I'm more likely to run up against a foreign language book or genealogical document. While Instant Camera Translation isn't always perfect, it can go a long way in overcoming these obstacles. Let's start with the basics.

How to use instant camera translation:

1. Point camera at text to translate
2. Works best on big, well-lit signs and menus (not as well on books or stylized text)
3. Tap SCAN button to translate text
4. Use your finger to highlight text
5. See the translation

In the photo on the next page, I'm using my tablet to conduct Instant Camera Translation on text that appears on my computer screen.

Here's a tip:

If you find the translation lacking, take a photo of the text for higher-quality translations.

Translation Example Step by Step

Now let's really put the app to work by using it in conjunction with one of my favorite free research tools: Google Books. With over 25 million books from around the world, and many of those fully digitized, Google Books is a gold mine for all genealogists. Follow along with me as I demonstrate an example of how the Google Translate app can work in conjunction with Google Books.

In this example, I'm in search of information on the town of Gladbeck, Germany, where my Great Grandparents once lived in the late 19th and early 20th century. But this time, rather than searching in my native language of English, I'm going to search for German books. To do that, my search query will need to be in German.

I tap the Google Translate app, and at the top of the screen, select from English to German.

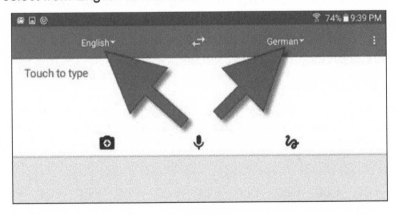

Next, I type the text "history of Gladbeck Germany" and tap the Done button on the keyboard. Instantly my query is translated into German as "Geschichte der Gladbeck Deutschland." I need a copy of this text, so I tap the copy icon and it is copied to the clipboard of my tablet.

Next, I head to my favorite web browser app and navigate to www.books.google.com. I press and hold in the search field, and tap Paste, and then tap the search button in Google books. Several books in the results list look promising, but I select *Evangelikale Beweung und evangelische Kirche in der Bundesrepublik*. I'm taken to page 686, on that page are many occurrences of the words I searched, highlighted in yellow. Along the right hand side of the page are small lines marking other pages that contain my search words.

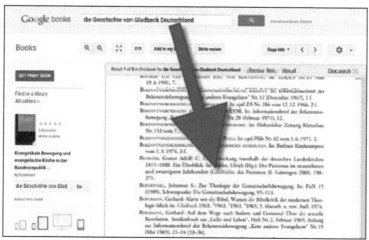

I head to the title page. Since I'm using my Android tablet for the example, I swipe the screen from right to left with the side of my palm to capture a screenshot. If I were using my iPad, I would press the home button and the power button simultaneously. (Check out the *Fabulous Mobile Tips and Tricks* chapter for more details on capturing screen shots.) The screen shot now resides in my photo gallery.

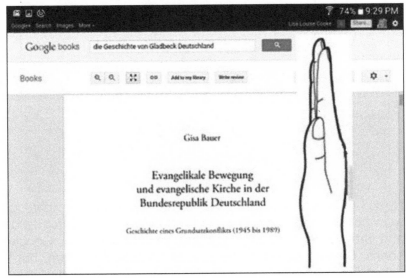

Back to the Google Translate app we go. But this time I'm going to change the language on the left at the top of the screen to English, and the language on the right (the one I want to translate *to*) to English. Rather than typing words, I'm going to tap the camera button. And instead of doing an instant translation in real time, I'm going to grab the screen shot from my photo gallery by tapping the images icon at the bottom of the screen.

In addition to screen shots you can also select images from your:

- Google Drive account
- Downloads
- Dropbox
- OneDrive
- Gallery / Photos

As soon as I tap the screen shot, Google Translate scans it (you'll see the scanner moving back and forth across the screen for a moment). If there's quite a bit of text on the page, you'll be prompted to highlight the text that you want translated by running your finger across it, or you can just tap Select All at the bottom of the screen.

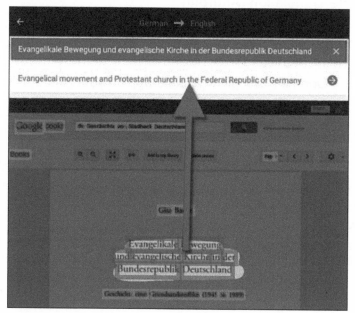

I see the German text is now captured above the image, and I press the translation button (right arrow in a blue circle) to get my results.

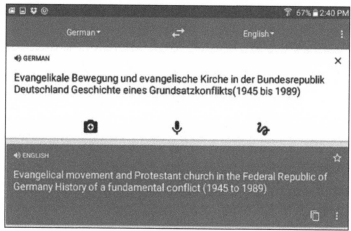

While this takes a bit of work, I've unearthed valuable information using this technique after exhausting my resources with English searches. Google Translate, in conjunction with your web browser, can bring a vast world of foreign language books to your research!

Offline Translation (Android)

When your internet connection is very slow, or expensive (such as when traveling internationally) Android users can download language packs to use offline. Here's how:

1. Open the Google Translate app on your Android device

2. Touch a language name at the top of the screen

3. Tap the download icon that appears to the right of the name of the language (If you don't see the download icon next to a language, it isn't available for download.)

4. When the language is done downloading, you'll see a check mark

Avoid potential delays or extra data usage charges by only downloading languages when you are using Wi-Fi. And bear in mind that not all offline languages can be used for instant camera translations.

Chapter 11: Travel

In the first edition of this book we discussed a few apps designed to help you organize your genealogy road trips. Several have been discontinued and are no longer available. Thankfully, travel is one of those tasks that can benefit from some app consolidation. It only takes one good note taking app to do the job of many apps. Evernote, One Note, and Google Keep all fit the bill. Each offer cloud synchronization between all of your computing devices, and the ability to include a variety of types of content giving you a lot of flexibility in your travel planning. Regardless of which you've selected as your primary note taking tool, here are some ideas for how to put them to work when you're hitting the road. (Note: In this section I'm going to use Evernote as my example, but the concepts apply to the other services as well.)

Tagging: Start off right by creating tags for your travel notes. I use a general Travel tag on all travel related notes, and then create a custom tag for individual trips (ex. Salt Lake 2016) Tag each note as you create it for easy retrieval as you need them.

Templates: Create travel related templates for notes you will be regularly using in your travel planning. Start by creating a master template note and tag it with Travel and Template. Then you can just make a copy of the template for use for a particular trip.

Here are some ideas for templates:

- Travel planning form
- Packing checklist
- Research plan notes
- Regularly Used Resources (including phone numbers, websites, etc.)

Reminders: There are always tasks along the way in travel planning, and reminders can help you stay on track. There are also those tasks that you need to do while on the road such as checking in for flights. For those airlines where the timing of checking in can put you at the front of the plane with adequate overhead bin space, or at the back with your carry-on bag stashed in the cargo hold, Reminders are the perfect solution. Don't rely on airline emails, let your note taking app put you at the front of the line.

1. Start by saving your fight confirmation to a note

2. Tap the Reminder icon

3. Select the date and time you wish to be notified

4. Tap Done

5. On the main screen your note will now be flagged as a reminder

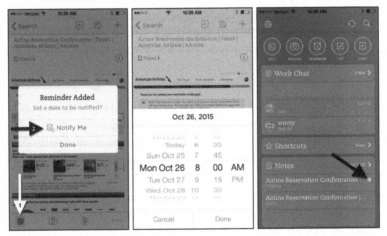

Be sure to activate notifications for the app in Settings so that you will receive your Reminder.

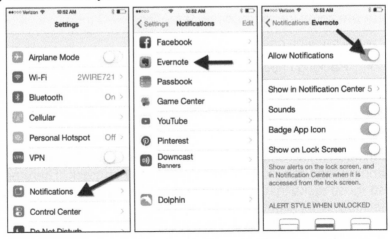

Notifications > Select the App > Slide "Allow Notifications" > Your Notification

If you have a paid subscription to Evernote (such as a Plus or Premium subscription) then you can send email to Evernote from your email account. An exclamation point in the subject line of a forwarded email turns the email into a Reminder in Evernote. You can set the Reminder up for a specific date using numeric values for year, month, and day, or you can just use a term such as 'tomorrow.'

Examples:

Email Subject: Airfare Reservation Check-in! 2014/06/26

Email Subject: Book hotel! tomorrow

Maps: A map with all your stops, airports, hotel, libraries and archives, etc. will reduce travel stress, and let you focus on research rather than directions. A Google Earth geographic "tour" map of your upcoming trip added to your notes is the perfect solution. (You can learn much more about using Google Earth specifically for genealogy in my book The Genealogist's Google Toolbox.)

Start by using the free Google Earth. I recommend doing this on your computer with the Google Earth Pro software, but you can create a basic tour with the Google Earth app on your tablet. (And of course you can always use SplashTop - see the chapter *Power Boost Your Tablet with Remote Access* - to access your computer and the software right from your tablet.)

In Google Earth, create a folder in your Places for your trip. Click this folder before adding each location to a tour map. Simply search for the location in the Search box, click the Placemark icon in the toolbar to mark the spot, and in the Place mark dialog box add a title and any pertinent information that will come in handy. Click OK to close the box and your place mark is complete. Here are some ideas for items to add to your map:

- Airports
- Hotels

- Restaurants

- Libraries, Archives, Historical Societies

- Ancestral Locations you want to visit

Here's an example of a Google Earth tour map that I created for a trip to Salt Lake City:

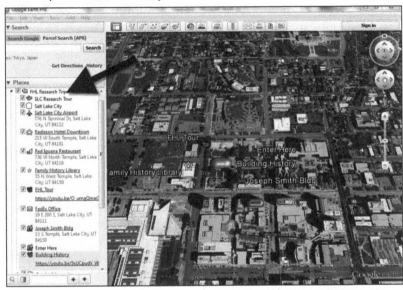

(Learn more about using Google Earth for genealogy by watching my free video class on my Genealogy Gems website: http://tinyurl.com/GoogleEarthFreeClass.)

When your map is complete, save it by right-clicking the tour folder and clicking Save Place As. Save it somewhere easy to find (I like Dropbox). Now you can simply drag and drop it onto a new note on your computer and it will appear on your mobile devices as well. You could also go straight to your mobile device, open the Dropbox app, and open the saved file in Evernote or Google Docs.

Happy and safe genealogical travels!

Chapter 12: Genealogy

Back when I first released The Genealogy Gems Podcast app there were just a handful of genealogy themed apps available. Today a search of the keyword "genealogy" delivers countless iPad and iPhone apps. However, not all apps are created equal.

Producers have various reasons for creating apps. Some apps provide unique and valuable ways to receive quality content on your tablet and phone, while others are essentially a vehicle for selling you genealogical content that may be of questionable value. For example, do you really need a $5 app to tell you the origin and meaning of your surname?

My goal in this chapter is to save you time and money by sharing with you the apps I have found to be of greatest genealogical value. This also means that I'm not covering more niche apps. However, I encourage you to regularly visit the App Store to conduct searches on keywords and phrases such as "genealogy," and "family history" to decide for yourself, as well as keep abreast of newly released apps.

Ancestry

by Ancestry.com

Price: Free

Available: App Store (including Apple Watch), Google Play

Ancestry is one of the most powerful genealogy websites under the family history big top, making their free app a logical choice for genealogists. The app provides you with access to Ancestry's vast collection of over 14 billion historical documents from the convenience of your mobile device, and features the Ancestry Hints TM tool. It also allows you to make discoveries through photographs, stories, and management of your online family tree. And the tools for managing your tree have expanded. Not only can you create and edit your family tree, but you can add family members directly from Facebook.

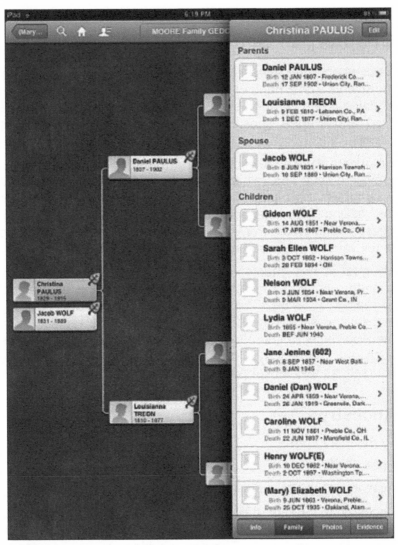

New features keep rolling out, with some of the more recent including the ability to receive notifications of new hints and comments, and if you've tested your DNA with Ancestry, you can explore your ethnic origins right in the app. Other new features include intuitive tools that give you the ability to resize profile images quickly. And now the iOS app allows you to take a shortcut to your Ancestry tree with a Spotlight search. From any Home screen page on your iPhone or iPad, touch your finger to the screen and drag down to reveal the Spotlight search field. Simply type Ancestry and hit Search. And finally, you can hide or show family events and Historical Insights to customize the LifeStory view. And with an internet connection, all of this synchronizes with your Ancestry.com account.

If you have an Apple watch you can receive new hint notifications with photo previews, save and ignore photo hints, keep up to date on comments and add voice dictated comments, and get on-this-day alerts for your family history events.

Of course you'll need a subscription to make full use of all the app's features. Subscription options include the U.S. Discovery and World Explorer plans, and keep in mind they are set to auto-renew.

MyHeritage

by MyHeritage.com

Price: Free

Available: App Store, Google Play

The MyHeritage app is growing in popularity around the world, and it's got a fresh new update which includes a completely redesigned version of the mobile app for iOS and Android. The enhanced app, with a better looking and more intuitive interface, allows you to:

- Build and synchronize your family tree with your MyHeritage.com account

- Fully sync with the Family Tree Builder software

- Search over 5 billion historical records (image)

- Preserve and share the information

You can even check out a fun celebrity look-alike feature (that could be a hoot at a family reunion and a good way to introduce relatives to your tree and the app!) There are over 20 million family trees on MyHeritage, and more than 4 million people worldwide have downloaded the MyHeritage app. And worldwide is the key word here: MyHeritage's strength is its global customer base. For example, the MyHeritage app is currently ranked in the top 5 apps in its category in Denmark and Norway in both Apple's App Store and Google Play. These are family historians who, like you, want to make connections. And this year the Android version was selected by Google as a 'featured app' in more than 100 countries. MyHeritage also supports 32 languages making it truly a global genealogy app particularly suited to international research.

Reunion for iPad

by Leister Productions, Inc.

Price: $14.99

Available: App Store

I'm not a Reunion user and I don't pretend to be. But anyone who is will want to get the Reunion for iPad app. It is designed for users of the genealogy database software Reunion 9.0c 0 on the Mac. According to the developer you must also have a wireless connection to your Mac for the app to be fully operational.

RootsMagic

by RootsMagic Ltd.

Price: Free

Available: App Store, Google Play

When it comes to doing genealogy research, a reliable genealogy software program is mandatory. One of the most popular on the market is RootsMagic. I've been a fan and user for a long time. Users will be thrilled to know that the RootsMagic app is now available for both iOS and Android. It lets you easily take your family history with you and view it on your tablet or smartphone.

The app enables you to put your actual RootsMagic family history files (rather than requiring you to convert them to a GEDCOM file format) on your device through iTunes or Dropbox. You'll be able to view your tree with Pedigree, Family, Descendant, and Individual Views, browse people by surname and given names, search by name or record number, and view media, notes, and sources for people, families, events, and facts.

Copying your files to your device using Dropbox is a two-step process.

Step 1: copying your file from the computer to Dropbox

Step 2: copying your file from Dropbox to your device.

How to copy your file from your computer to Dropbox:

1) Open your file in RootsMagic on your computer

2) From the menu, click File > Save to Dropbox for Apps

3) Sign in to Dropbox with your Dropbox account and give it permission to upload your file

How to copy your file from Dropbox to your device:

1) In the RootsMagic app, select the "File" option

2) Select the "Dropbox" option that appears

(Note: If you haven't previously connected to Dropbox from the RootsMagic app, you will be directed to Dropbox to sign in. Dropbox will ask you to authorize the RootsMagic app. Click the "Allow" button to authorize the RootsMagic app. A folder called "Apps" will be created in the root of your Dropbox Folder. Inside of the "Apps" folder will be created a "RootsMagic" directory.)

3) From the list, select your file. (It may take a minute or so to download depending on the size of the file. A message will pop up when the file is finished downloading to let you know you are ready to use the database.)

4) The file should appear under the "On Device" tab in the RootsMagic app.

Your file has now been copied to your device. It doesn't need to be reloaded from Dropbox unless you change the file on your computer. If you edit the database on your computer (and re-save it to Dropbox as above), the RootsMagic app will let you know that the files have been modified, and need to be re-downloaded to your device.

The app also includes the following tools:

- Perpetual calendar
- Date calculator
- Relationship calculator
- Soundex calculator

If you use other genealogy software such as PAF, Family Tree Maker, Legacy Family Tree, you can convert your files into viewable RootsMagic files using the free RootsMagic Essentials desktop software.

It's not as robust (yet) as they Ancestry app. You will still need your RootsMagic desktop genealogy software or the free RootsMagic Essentials software to create, edit, or add to your genealogy files. But I would guess that we will continue to see increased functionality added into the future. Michael Booth, vice-president at RootsMagic puts it this way, "We see this as our first step into the mobile world. We're interested in seeing how people use this app and evolving it to meet their needs."

Families

by TelGen Limited

Price: $14.99

Available: App Store, Google Play

Legacy Family Tree software has a very strong following of devoted users. The roots of this genealogy database go all the way back to a software program called Generations, which also happens to be the first program I ever used. Today Legacy Family Tree is far more robust, feature-packed, and now has its own app. All this makes the Families app a must-have for anyone who uses the software.

Families makes it possible for your Legacy Family Tree family files to be easily transferred to your mobile device where they can be not only viewed, but also edited. Here's a run-down of just some of the functionality you'll have access to with this app:

- Create new family files from scratch
- Work on existing files and multiple family files
- Access Family View, Pedigree View, Descendant View and Timeline
- Index, searchable by given name, surname or RIN
- Events
- To do lists
- Master and detail sources
- Locations and addresses, with geolocation via Google Maps
- Alternate names
- Pictures from your camera or photo album
- Documents, audio and video files
- Bookmarks
- Portrait and landscape mode in all views
- Full screen support on the iPad

Even if your family tree is huge (lucky you!), Families can handle it. The developers say the app uses a highly efficient "database implementation" allowing very large family files to be supported.

You'll need to have Legacy Family Tree software running on your PC in order to transfer family files to and from the iPhone, iPod Touch, iPad or Android device. There isn't currently a Mac version of Legacy Family Tree, but the developers say that Legacy will run on newer Macs with Windows installed under Bootcamp, Parallel or Fusion.

A free program called Families Sync, which can be downloaded from http://www.telgen.co.uk/families/ is required to transfer your files using a Wi-Fi network connection or a USB cable between the device and the PC. You will also need to have the free iTunes program installed on your PC. You can also use Families Sync just to convert your family file to and from the format required by Families, and transfer the file using email or a cloud-based service like Dropbox. Don't let all this techie talk deter you. Legacy Family Tree has a wonderful free webinar video for you to watch explaining it all from the folks who know it best. You can watch it for free at http://tinyurl.com/familieswebinar.

Family Tree

by FamilySearch

Price: Free

Available: App Store, Google Play

FamilySearch.org is a must-visit free genealogy website, which makes the Family Tree by FamilySearch app a must-have app. It brings your entire online FamilySearch family tree to your mobile device, synchronizing it with each edit and addition you make. You'll also enjoy adding photos and stories to the branches of your tree, adding richness to the experience.

Start by signing up for a free account at www.familysearch.org and then sign in to that account on the app. The first screen is your Pedigree Chart, which you can resize easily with your fingers. Tap an individual on the tree to access their information. Source information appears giving you the important background on the origin of your data.

You'll find a menu across the top of the app which you can slide to the left to reveal more options such as:

- Spouse – Add children or additional spouses
- Parents – Add parents and siblings
- Sources – Where your information comes from
- Photos – Attach photos to your tree and tag them
- Stories – Add stories by typing or dictation
- Charts – Create PDF chart files

You can locate additional records on the FamilySearch website by tapping the three dots icon on any individual's record and tap Search Records. Tap the Attach to Family Tree button on any record to add it to your tree.

If you need a little help using the app, tap the three horizontal lines icon at the top of the screen. There beginners will find a terrific Quick Start feature that will prompt them through the process of building a family tree. Or tap Help to access answers to frequently asked questions and support.

FamilySearch Memories

by FamilySearch.org

Free

Available: App Store, Google Play

If you have a family tree on the free Family Search website, you're going to love using Memories. And if you don't yet have a tree on the site, this app may convince you to do so. It provides an easy and thoroughly enjoyable way to balance the various types of family history content that comes your way and bring it together. You can add photographs, stories and audio recordings to your tree, and build a legacy of family history content.

You will need a FamilySearch account to get started. If you don't already have an account, head to www.familysearch.org to sign up. The beauty of this app is that it will synchronize with your FamilySearch account when you are connected to the internet. And, in the absence of an internet connection, you will still have convenient access to all of your data while on the go.

Next, download the app and tap the gear icon to go to the Settings to log in to your account. Here you will also find the Help section where you can get answers to your questions about how to use the app, see what's new, and provide feedback.

Photos

Start by adding some old family photos, but don't stop there. Snap images of genealogical documents and anything else noteworthy with your mobile device to add them to Memories.

How to add a photo:

1. Tap Photos
2. Tap the plus/circle icon
3. Select an image from your device or take a photo (you will need to grant the app permission to access your camera and photos)
4. Edit the photo as desired with the crop and rotate tool
5. Tap Save (Notice that when you are connected to the Internet, the app will automatically synchronize your work with your FamilySearch account.)
6. To tag the people in the image, tap the image
7. Tap the Who is this about? icon
8. Tap the circle on the first person's face
9. Tap Add a Name
10. Start to type the name in the name field. If the name appears in your family tree it will appear in the list.
11. Tap Done

Stories

The Stories feature is a wonderful way to collect details about the photos you've added to your tree and anything else that enriches your family history. In addition to stories, expand your storytelling to favorite family jokes and sayings. Not a big fan of typing on your device's small keyboard? Tap the microphone key and dictate your story. Then flesh out your stories by adding applicable photos. Since you are working in your account, the story is attributed to you, and Memories will include the date that you created it.

How to add a story:

1. Tap Stories
2. Tap the plus/circle icon
3. Tap Enter Story Title and give your story a title
4. Tap Enter Story Content to add your story with the keyboard or dictate with the microphone
5. Tap to add a photo if you wish
6. Tap Done
7. Tap the Who is this about icon at the top to add the story to people in your FamilySearch family tree.
8. Type in a name or pick from the existing tree list
9. Tap Done

Audio

Finally, don't miss the Audio tool. Use it to interview family members and record audio memories of your own such as:

- Favorite memories
- A Childhood Adventure
- What you admired most about your Dad

How to record a memory:

1. Tap Audio
2. Tap the plus/circle icon (the first time you use this feature you will be promoted to allow the app to access your device's microphone. Just tap OK)
3. Tap the microphone to record
4. Tap Done
5. Enter a title
6. Tap OK
7. Your recording now appears in the Audio section of the app

How to delete an audio recording:

1. Tap Audio

2. Tap the recording you wish to delete

3. Tap the 3 dot icon in the upper right corner of the recording

4. Tap Delete Recording (you can also edit the title at this point)

5. Tap Delete in the popup window

Chapter 13: Education & Information

I'm a big advocate of ongoing genealogical education. I believe to make the best use of your time and get the best results you need to keep updating your skills. This is particularly true when it comes to using technology for genealogy.

Staying up to speed isn't as easy as it sounds. There's a lot of "information noise" these days. My Genealogy Gems podcast and website (www.genealogygems.com) sprung out of a desire to help filter the noise and distill it down to what I consider to be the best "gems" for you and your genealogy research.

We all learn differently however. Some of us need to read information, some need to hear it, and others want to see it. We do all three at Genealogy Gems (blog, videos, and audio podcast). We've already covered reading blogs, so in this chapter we'll cover audio and video.

Podcasts (Audio)

Apple Podcasts App

by Apple

Price: Free

Available: App Store

Android Alternatives: Podbean, Stitcher and BeyondPod

In the Podcasts App you can explore hundreds of thousands of free audio and video podcasts from the iTunes Podcasts Catalog.

I was thrilled to find that when I opened the app for the first time the podcasts I subscribe to in iTunes on my PC were already there.

Try the Featured section to find new podcasts on a wide range of topics, and subscribe right from within the app to receive new free episodes when they are released. The app allows you to stream episodes, or download them to listen without

Internet connection. Playback controls allow you skip forward and backward, and there's a Sleep Timer that automatically stops playing the episode while you are listening in bed.

Genealogy Gems

by Wizzard Media

Featuring *The Genealogy Gems Podcast*

Price: $2.99

Available: App Store, Google Play

The Genealogy Gems Podcast app was one of the very early genealogy apps on the scene, and was included in App Advice's Top iPad Apps for Hobbies list as a "must have app" for genealogy. One of the reasons I was so anxious to make an app available on mobile devices was because so many of my listeners tell me they are on the go while they listen. Streaming the free podcast from the mobile app is much simpler and easier than the old method of plugging an iPod into your computer and downloading episodes through iTunes!

The app automatically searches for and downloads the newest episodes, and it plays in the background while you use your phone or tablet for other things (like genealogy research.)

Another advantage of the app is the special and exclusive bonus content that we tuck into episodes. Look for the "e" icon (image) on the episode screen which indicates that bonus content is available for that episode. Tap the "e" icon to access and enjoy the extra audio or video content.

The app also features the ability to visit our Genealogy Gems website, flag favorite episodes, and share episodes through Facebook, Twitter, and Email.

Video

YouTube

by Google

Price: Free

Available: App Store, Google Play

Video is the fastest growing segment of online content. In addition to funny cat videos, this is due in large part to the growth of educational videos. Video offers educators a compelling way to show and tell how-to information. Want to find out how to merge duplicate trees on Ancestry? In YouTube search for *how to merge duplicate Ancestry Tree* and you'll get at least four videos showing you how. If you want to find out how to do something, YouTube can often present faster, more exacting answers than a Google search.

YouTube is a free service (owned by Google) for sharing your own videos, or watching genealogy themed videos produced by others. For example, you'll find over 90 educational videos at my Genealogy Gems YouTube Channel at www.youtube.com/genealogygems. Other big names with YouTube channels include Ancestry, FamilySearch, Family Tree Magazine, and the National Archives. There's also a paid version called Red that allows you to watch YouTube with no advertising (https://www.youtube.com/red).

In addition to educational videos, believe it or not, there's a lot of family history to be found on YouTube. I cover this topic regularly on the Genealogy Gems blog. Here's a link that will give you all of my blog posts covering YouTube in chronological order, starting with the most recent:

http://lisalouisecooke.com/category/youtube-2/

You'll also find a full chapter on the subject in my book *The Genealogist's Google Toolbox.*

Chapter 14:
Captivating Non-Genealogists

It's a problem all family historians face – how to get non-genealogist family members interested in the family history. It is natural to want to share discoveries that we find exciting about ancestors we have in common, but for non-genealogist relatives it can be a ho-hum proposition. They don't see family history as we do. In my live presentation *How to Captivate the Non-Genealogists in Your Life* that I give to genealogy audiences here and abroad (yep, it's a challenge faced by genealogists around the world!) I stress the importance of presenting family history in a way that speaks to and captivates those family members.

Your iPad is one of your strongest allies in this endeavor, and here are some apps that can go a long way to helping you present family history in a fascinating way.

Pic Collage

by Cardinal Blue Software

Price: Free

Available: App Store, Google Play

It's amazing that I finished writing this book at all considering how easily distracted I became while I was researching all these great apps. Pic Collage was one of the biggest culprits! It's just plain fun to use, and creates attractive, shareable collages quickly. And over the years, new features have been added.

Start by tapping to select the type of image you want to create on the home screen: Grid patterns, templates, or freestyle. Next, tap the plus sign to add photos from your device's Camera Roll / Gallery, your Facebook account, or websites. Then jazz up your collage by adding text (with font and color options), a new background, or stickers. It comes with a small collection of free stickers and offers additional styles for purchase. But you really don't need to worry about buying stickers because with the ability to grab photos from the web you also have the ability to grab clip art and other types of images. Just be sure to check the image for rights of use.

We love you Uncle Buzz!

Editing and manipulating your images is easy. If you add an image you don't want, just swipe it off the screen. To rotate, just grab the image with two fingers and turn. One tap of the image brings it to the forefront, and double tapping provides you with an editing menu for even more customization.

When your collage is complete, sharing in a variety of ways is a breeze. Collages are perfect for sharing you on Facebook, and you can also post it on Twitter, save it to your tablet's camera roll, or send it as a postcard or email it.

This app offers a quick and easy method for creating a digital scrapbook that you can share spontaneously when you have a chance meeting with a distant cousin. A collage would make a wonderful "can't wait to see you" reminder postcard for an upcoming family reunion. The possibilities are endless. And the app is simple enough that you could pull your grandkids up on your lap and have them create their own family history collage. Picture this: the kids pick out a picture from your camera roll and add it to their collage while you tell them a story about that ancestor.

Google Earth

by Google, Inc.

Price: Free

Available: App Store, Google Play

Those who have listened to *The Genealogy Gems Podcast* have heard me say many times that I think Google Earth is one of the most powerful software programs for genealogy, and yet it is NOT a genealogy program! When you consider the fact that genealogy revolves around location, it makes a lot of sense that a robust location-based tech tool like Google Earth would come in handy. Currently, however, the free Google Earth app is a somewhat stripped down version of the desktop program. Don't let that stop you from downloading it. It's very effective for searching locations around the globe, and is capable of displaying fairly complex Google Earth files.

For example, in my Google Earth for Genealogy video CD series I teach how to use the computer version of Google Earth to create multi-media rich maps that I call "family history tours." In these map tours you "fly" to each place of ancestral significance on the map revealing relevant videos, family photos, genealogical documents and more.

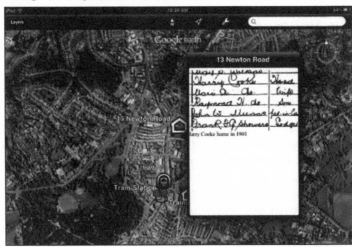

You can also record it all with the built-in screen capture tool and your computer's microphone. The final result is a tour that brings family history to life, and even looks a bit like a cool computer video game to the kids.

Google Earth maps and tours are saved as .KMZ files. And that's where the app comes in. All .KMZ files can be beautifully displayed on your mobile device with the app. In the previous edition of this book I explained that the Google Earth app wasn't able to open these files, and a second app called KMZ Loader was required. Thankfully, those days are gone, and the Google Earth app is now capable of opening KMZ files. So whether you create your own files, or find one while browsing online, you can tap it and launch it in the Google Earth app.

After creating your family history tour on your computer, save it to Dropbox or another similar cloud-based file storage app. (Refer back to the chapter on File Storage & Management for a refresher on cloud-based file storage apps.) The file will synchronize via your internet connection, and become available on your mobile device in the Dropbox app.

How to share KMZ files via Dropbox:

1. Create the file on your computer
2. Save the file to Dropbox
3. Tap the Dropbox app on your tablet
4. Tap the KMZ file
5. Tap the Share icon
6. Tap "Open In"
7. Select Open in Google Earth and the Google Earth app will open and display the file

While currently the Google Earth app offers only a fraction of the capabilities that the full-blown desk top version does, it is perfect for sharing your tours while on the road. It is one thing to show a relative a photo of Great Grandpa's village in England, but it's quite another to "fly" them there with Google Earth, and click on icons revealing Great Grandpa's photo, the census record, and a video about the area or his profession. (Add your home movies to YouTube and you can include those too!) Learn more about how to use Google Earth for genealogy by watching my free video class *Google Earth for Genealogy* at http://tinyurl.com/GoogleEarthFreeClass.

The Google Earth app isn't totally stripped down. You can also access various Layers in the app to get an enhanced view of any location. Tap the three horizontal lines icon to reveal the available options such as Borders and Labels, Roads and 3D Buildings.

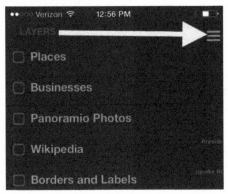

Google is continually improving the app. Check frequently for updates in the App Store so that you can enjoy all the new features.

Pinterest

by Pinterest, Inc.

Price: Free

Available: App Store, Google Play

Pinterest is a hot name in social media these days. It reminds me a lot of the bulletin boards and memory books we used to have in college. Maybe it was just a girl thing, but my friends and I would cut pictures out of magazines and glue them into blank books as a collection of 'favorite things' to inspire us, and to dream about.

Today you can collect your favorite online things and share them with your friends and relatives through Pinterest. If you see something you like on a website, you can pin it to your virtual Pinterest board. Your pins are assembled in a slick magazine type format that makes the most of your tablet's glorious display.

While Pinterest lends itself to home decorating and recipes, genealogists have definitely jumped on the pinning bandwagon. They collect and share their favorite family photos, display ideas, motivational sayings, and much more. Creative display ideas are a particularly popular topic. Visit my "family history" boards at http://pinterest.com/lisalouisecooke.

THIS DAY in My Family History

by Kaik3 / Michael Holt

Price: $0.99

Available: App Store, Google Play

Here's a simple yet fun app that dishes up all the events that happened on this day in your family history, and how you are related to the people involved.

Has an ancestor's story been on the backburner a little too long? This app could be just the nudge you need to go back and pick up that research, it works great as a writing prompt. And of course it's always fun to get nostalgic with living relatives. They will be blown away at your incredible memory when you remind them it is the anniversary of a particular family event.

You'll be prompted to log into and connect with your free FamilySearch account.

Select how many generations you want to include up to six, and tap Download Ancestry. Tap Settings to select which events you want included: Birth, Death, Marriage, and Other. If there's no event for a particular day, the app tells you simply to "do some family history!"

Little Family Tree

by Yellow Fork Technologies LLC

Price: $3.99

Available: Google Play (iOS in 2016)

This app uses your FamilySearch family tree to set up engaging games and puzzles for the toddlers and preschoolers in your family. There are matching games for names and faces and photo puzzles. The clever Heritage Dress Up Game calculates the child's heritage makeup based on the current known information in your family tree on FamilySearch. When a nationality is selected, an ancestor from that place appears providing a more personal connection to that heritage. A paper doll character is displayed sporting the traditional dress of the location. Tap Play and your child can dress the doll.

The Little Family Tree app is an interactive introduction to genealogy for the next generation.

Part Three: Become a Power User

Chapter 15: Power Boost Your Tablet: Remote Access

Now that you have a great collection of apps you are ready to power boost your tablet by dramatically expanding its capabilities and reach. You can do that through remote access to your desktop computer.

As I mentioned at the beginning of this book, it's important to develop a "Tablet Mindset," understanding that a tablet is not a desktop or laptop computer. There are things that your computer at home can do that a tablet can't. However, with remote access all of those programs and capabilities are available to you on your tablet.

When you use a remote desktop app, **you are turning your tablet into a terminal that can operate your desktop computer**. This opens a whole new world of computing on your tablet! With remote access you no longer have to worry about how you are going to enter data into your genealogy program while on the road. You can do it on your home computer through your tablet.

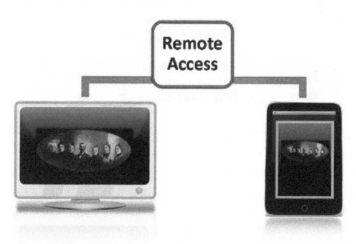

As a speaker, I travel to genealogy groups all over the country. That means I'm often away from my desktop computer. I have accomplished all of the following tasks on my home computer with just my iPad and a remote desktop app:

- Created and edited PowerPoint presentations
- Published podcast episodes
- Created videos and uploaded them to YouTube
- Created Google Earth family history tours
- Printed items to my home printer

and that's just a sampling.

Now you may be thinking "that's great, but how do I get those documents I'm creating on my home computer while I'm on the road?" One word: Dropbox.

I hope by now you have signed up for your free Dropbox account (or similar service). A cloud storage service is indispensable for working with remote access. Once you have Dropbox on your home computer and have downloaded the app to your tablet, you have the ability to share documents back and forth by simply dragging and dropping them into the Dropbox folder. Dropbox will then synchronize the files and make them available on all of your computing devices that have Dropbox installed.

Until now, I have always recommended SplashTop Personal as my preferred remote access app. It was one of the first available, one of the most affordable at the time, and I found it to be very reliable. That has all changed.

Chrome Remote Desktop is my new preferred remote access app. Here's why:

- It's free (that's hard to beat!)
- I've found the clarity of the transmitted screen to be superior to SplashTop
- It was easier to set up
- It works on the same WiFi network in the same house, or on a different WiFi network on the road
- It has a virtual mouse that works more like a real mouse
- It works on Android and Apple devices
- It now works on Macs as well as PC

- It includes Remote Assistant, allowing you to share your computer with someone else

What's not to love?

Chrome Remote Desktop

By Google

Price: Free

Available: App Store, Google Play

The Chrome Remote Desktop app allows you to access your home computer with your mobile device, and it also allows you to share your computer with someone else (called Remote Assistant). We'll start with remotely accessing your computer.

Remote Access

How to set up Chrome Remote Desktop:

1. **On the computer that you want to access**, open the Chrome web browser, or install Chrome at https://www.google.com/chrome/browser/desktop/. Then sign in or create a free Google account.

2. Go to the Google Chrome Store at https://chrome.google.com/webstore and search for *Chrome Remote Access.*

3. Click the Add to Chrome button and follow the installation instructions.

4. Chrome Remote Access will be added to your Google Apps. You can access your Google Apps by going to www.google.com and clicking the icon that looks like 3x3 rows of squares. When I installed it, a Google Apps icon was added to my system tray at the bottom of my screen which is very handy! Just click it to see all the apps including Remote Access.

5. Click Chrome Remote Access to launch it.

6. You'll be presented with two options: Remote Assistance or My Computers. Click the button for My Computers.

7. You'll be prompted to Enable Remote Connections (click the button) and then click the Run button.

8. Then you'll be prompted to set up a pin number made up of 6 or more digits and sign in.

9. Finally, a pop up window will notify you that remote connections for your computer have been enabled. You'll also be advised to check your computer's power-saving settings in your computer's Control Panel to allow for remote access. If you're not sure where to find them in the Control Panel, type *Power Saving* in the Control Panel search box.

10. On your mobile device, go to the app store and download the free Chrome Remote Access app.

11. Sign in with your free Google account.

12. You'll see your computer listed on the MyComputers page. Tap it and sign in with the same pin you set up on your computer.

13. You are now accessing your computer using your tablet or smart phone!

Now your mobile devices are truly as powerful as your desktop computer! Remote access has revolutionized mobile computing. Once you use remote access a couple of times you'll likely wonder how you ever lived without it. And as an added bonus, this works computer to computer as well.

The app is pretty straightforward. Here are the highlights:

End your remote access session

Tap the Back arrow (Android) or X (iOS) in the upper left corner. On Android you can also tap the 3 vertical dots icon and tap Disconnect.

Keyboard

Tap the keyboard icon to open the keyboard, allowing you to type on your home computer. Tap it again to close the keyboard.

Full Screen

Tap the bracketed square icon for full screen. To exit full screen mode, tap the upper right corner of the black bar at the top of the screen.

Help

Tap the 3 vertical dots icon and tap Help & Feedback

Remote Assistant

Since Remote Assistant is part of Chrome Remote Assistant I'm going to explain it here, even though it is a computer to computer function.

Have you ever needed technical help, called a friend or relative, and tried to follow along with their instructions? Wouldn't it be nice to be able to just give them access to your computer so that they can fix the problem and you can watch them do it? Or how about when you're collaborating on a genealogy research project? In the past I have helped students via email with projects like creating a family history tour in Google Earth. There are times it would have been much easier just to be able to access their computer to work directly on their project rather than emailing large files back and forth or trying to explain the instructions in a text email. Remote Assistant accomplishes the task of collaboration!

Before we get started, keep in mind that when you use the app to share your computer with another person, that person will see your email address and have full control of your computer. This includes having access to your applications, files, emails, documents and history. So please, share with caution and with people you know and trust because you do so at your own risk.

How to use Remote Assistant:

1. In Chrome, open a new tab.

2. In the toolbar (or in your task tray) click the Apps icon.

3. Open the Chrome Remote Desktop app.

4. Click the Get Started button under "Remote Assistance".

5. Click the Share button. (Both users must be running the Chrome Remote Desktop app so make sure the other person has it installed as well.)

6. A unique access code will be generated for each sharing session. Send this code to the person you want to share your computer with. For privacy reasons you may want to call the person and give it to them over the phone rather than emailing it.

7. Once the other user enters the access code, the sharing session will begin and he or she will be able to

see your computer screen. You can click Stop Sharing or   press Ctrl+Alt+Esc (Mac:Opt-Ctrl-Esc)   at any time to end the session.

How to access a computer that has been shared with you on your computer:

1. In Chrome, open a new tab

2. Click Apps ⦂⦂⦂ on the Chrome bar. (According to Google, if you are using Windows 8, you can only access a shared computer on the Desktop mode.)

3. Click the Access button.

4. Enter the access code provided by the other person.

5. Click Connect.

6. Your email address will be displayed to the user who has shared his/her computer with you.

Chapter 16: Mobile Tips & Tricks

You may have noticed that your tablet came with very few instructions, even though it is packed with special features. The following tips and tricks will help you do more with increased efficiency – and have a lot of fun too!

As you may recall, the first edition of this book was focused on the iPad. In this edition we have a more global perspective on mobile devices generally. But as you can imagine, with all the variations of devices and operating systems, that is a tall order! Let's keep our eye on the **concepts and functionality** and continue talking about how you can use your device for genealogy.

I will be addressing the iPad first, and then will add comparable information on Android. Since it isn't possible to provide instructions for every single combination of device / operating system, once you read about what the possibilities are, **I strongly encourage you to:**

- **go to Settings** (Android) or Search (iOS) and run a keyword search on the function or item I'm discussing to pinpoint its location on your particular device.

- **check the Help features** on your device to see if your tablet or smartphone can do the same thing.

- **run a Google search.** Here's an example of a Google search for finding information applicable to your device: *Samsung Tab 4 Android 5.0 "split keyboard"* (For more help with crafting productive Google search queries read my book *The Genealogist's Google Toolbox*.)

- **check that your device's operating system is up to date.** It is the engine behind many of these techniques. Refer to the chapter *A Few Tips for Using This Book* for instructions on how to check that your operating system is up to date.

- **check your app store.** Search on keywords associated with the function you desire and you may discover that there is an app out there that can do the trick.

New Features

Because some significant new features have become available on the new iPad and version of iOS, I'm going to address those first. These features focus on multitasking and productivity. And Android users, don't be surprised to see similar features coming to an Android device near you in the future. In the next section we'll go back to features more readily found on both Android and iOS.

Note that some of these features are only functional on newer devices. Specifically, the Split Screen feature is only available on iPad Air 2, iPad mini 4, iPad Pro and newer.

You should also take note that not all apps have updated to take advantage of the new features so some of your favorites might not be able to perform these tasks yet. Apps are quickly catching up though, so keep checking for updates in the App Store.

Slide Over

Slide over allows you to open a second app in a sidebar without leaving the one you're in. To do this, swipe from right to left on the right side of your iPad. Then select an app to open by tapping it. To switch to a different app, swipe from the top down. Slide Over freezes the app you have open on the left, so the best use of this feature is for a quick task such as checking your email.

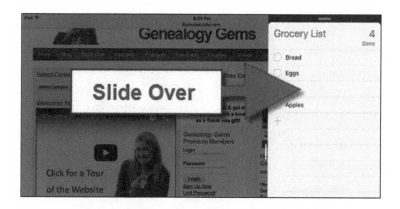

Split View

With Split View, you can have two apps open and active at the same time. Open a second app as a Slide Over, then press and hold on the divider between the two apps and drag it to the center of the screen. You now have two apps open and functioning.

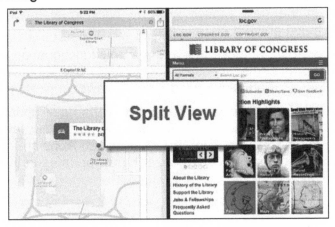

Picture in Picture

You can use Picture in Picture while using FaceTime or watching a video. While watching a video in full screen, press the Home button and the video will scale down to a corner of your display. Now when you tap to open and use a second app your video will continue to play. You can move the small video screen to different corners by dragging it.

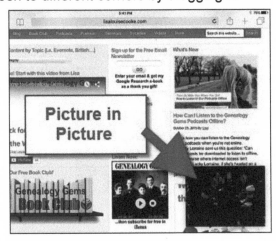

QuickType

There have been some new improvements to the QuickType keyboard. At the top of the keyboard you will find buttons to quickly add an attachment, copy/paste, and format the text. Another new feature is that you can now use the keyboard as a track pad. Swipe over the keyboard with two fingers and you will be able to control your cursor, making it easier to select portions of text.

Keyboard and Gesture Tips and Tricks

iOS and Android equivalents

My motto is *"saving time with tech, means more time with ancestors."*

To that end, these tips and tricks will save you little bits here and there, adding up to a lot of time saved. And besides, these techniques are just more convenient to use.

To take advantage of some of the following features, the first thing you will need to do is go into Settings > Keyboard and turn on the various features you find there such as:

- Auto-Capitalization
- Auto-Correction
- Enable Cap Lock
- Shortcuts
- Predictive
- Split Keyboard
- "." Shortcut

Enable Caps Lock

No longer do you have to tap the shift key every time you want to type a letter in an all caps word. Tap the Shift key twice to activate cap lock (the Shift key will turn blue indicating that cap lock is on) then type away. Tap the Shift key once again to turn off cap lock. This works on Android as well.

"." Shortcut

Considering how much typing we do, this little time saver will add up to more research time over the long haul.

Double space at the end of a sentence and the iPad will automatically place a period and one space, ready for the next sentence.

Split Keyboard

Have you noticed how fast some people can text with their thumbs? And this type of typing allows them to hold their device (usually a smartphone) while typing. With a tablet this gets really tricky. We usually have to set it on our lap or balance it in one hand while typing with the other. Being able to split your keyboard allows you to bring the speed and stability of texting to your tablet.

iOS

Whenever the keyboard is visible in an app, **firmly grasp your tablet with two hands**, and place your two thumbs together at the center of the keyboard. Swipe outwards in opposite directions. (Remember, hold on tight!) This will split the keyboard, making it easier to hold the iPad in two hands while typing – much like texting – with your thumbs.

When done, simply place your thumbs on the outer edges of the keyboard and swipe the two pieces of the keyboard inward, back together again.

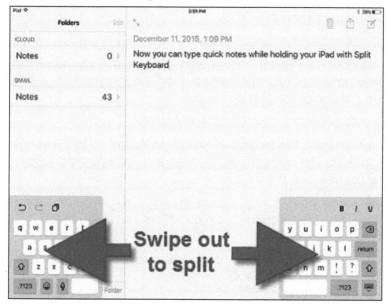

This doesn't work on your smartphone, because you don't need it on your phone's much smaller screen.

Android

While this could vary by device, on my Android tablet split keyboard is activated but pressing and holding the key next to the spacebar. It may appear as a gear icon (Settings) or microphone. Tap the keyboard styles key and you can not only select split keyboard, but also a floating keyboard.

There are free apps in Google Play that provide Android users with split keyboard functionality. Search for *split keyboard.*

Hidden Keyboard Characters

When you first look at the keyboard it may seem a bit incomplete. Not so – there are additional characters hidden throughout! Here's the run down on which key to press and hold in order to get the character you are looking for on the iPad:

Foreign Characters

Tap and hold A, E, I, O, U, Y, S, L, Z, C, N and you will get the corresponding foreign characters for those letters.

On Android head to Settings > Language to select foreign language keyboards.

Numbers and Symbols Board

Hold down 0, hyphen, dollar sign, ampersand, question mark, exclamation mark, apostrophe, and quotes to find a wider array of corresponding symbols.

Quick Apostrophe and Quotation Marks

Save yourself the trouble of switching to the ".?123" keyboard to look for the apostrophe, and do a quick upwards swipe on the comma key. It's a big time saver!

The same goes for quotation marks. Give a quick upwards swipe to the Period/Question Mark key to quickly add quotation marks.

Android users will find suggested symbols and spellings across the top of the tablet's keyboard.

Em Dash & Bullets

I love my bulleted lists – and I enjoy using em dashes too! On my Samsung (Android) tablet they are built into my keyboard. But that isn't the case on all Android devices, and it's not currently the case on iOS. Here's how to create them on your tablet and smart phone. Tap and hold the dash key to reveal a menu that includes the em dash, a bullet key, and the underscore.

Italicized Quotation Marks and Brackets

Tap and hold the quotation mark key to reveal italicized quotes and brackets. Press lightly if you have a new iPhone. If you press too hard you will trigger the pop-out feature, but there will be nothing to pop-out. Just lightly press and hold and the additional menu will appear. And as with the em dash and bullets, these are included in my Android tablet's keyboard. If you don't see them on your device, give this tip a try.

Magnifying Glass

You may have noticed when you are typing on your iPad that it can be a bit tricky trying to place the cursor at an exact point in a line of text in order to make a correction. The Magnifying Glass feature solves this problem.

Press your finger on the screen and hold it there to activate the circular magnifying glass. Drag your finger along the line of text and you will see the cursor follow along. This will allow you to place the cursor at the exact spot – even in the middle of a word – where you want to make a correction.

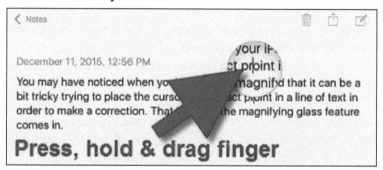

Release your finger and a menu will appear that allows you to Select and Select All. Tap either and points will appear giving you control over the text that you are selecting and providing you with a more extensive menu of options including cut and paste, formatting, sharing the text, and insert photo.

Android: My experience on my Android tablet is that there is more control when tapping the screen to select your starting point, making this feature really not necessary. Pressing and holding text brings up a menu featuring Select all, Cut, Copy and Paste, Clipboard and Dictionary.

Navigation Tips and Tricks

A Quick Look at Your Day

If you have items in your device's calendar, use the Messages app, or have notifications activated for other apps, they will pop up at the top of your screen to notify you. But there's a quick way to access updates any time you need them.

Place your finger on the header bar at the top of the screen (the one that shows the time and the battery) and swipe downward. This will reveal your items for today and your notifications.

I love this swiping feature because I live by my Google Calendar. I linked my Google Calendar into the iPad's Calendar app by signing into Calendar with my Gmail address (both Gmail and Calendar are tied to the same free account). This means that I no longer have to open my Google App or the Calendar app to check my appointments.

Scroll Back

Sometimes when you are viewing a very long webpage of genealogical data, a spreadsheet, or other long document, you will want to return to the top of the page. You could swipe your finger multiple times making your way back up to the top, but there is an easier way.

To quickly scroll back to the top of a page simply tap the bar across the top of the screen that displays the time and battery life. This is a time saver to start using right away.

Android: Sorry, but this feature appears to be iOS specific.

Quick Closing apps

There's more to navigation than swiping with a single finger. These next two tricks occur when you activate *Gestures*. (Settings > General > Gestures)

The first is a really quick way to close an app. Place your outstretched fingers and thumb on the screen and pinch inwards. This will quickly close the app that you currently have open.

Android: This technique doesn't work with Android. However, there's a great article on Wiki How featuring multiple ways to close apps. You'll find it at http://www.wikihow.com/Close-Apps-on-Android.

By the way, even when you use the multi-finger close described above, or press the Home button at the bottom of the screen to close, the app is still running in the background. While you are in an open app, you can scroll between all the apps you currently have open by dragging four fingers to the right or left on the screen. This comes in really handy when you are juggling tasks, and saves lots of time.

The Multitasking Screen

Want to get back to where you were recently? Double press the home button and the apps you accessed most recently will appear. Swipe left and right to scroll through the apps. To close the dock, press the home button once more. You'll never get lost again!

While you are in the multitasking screen, you can also close apps (or "force quit" when an app isn't working properly). To do this, swipe to the app you want to close, then slide the app "card" to the top of the screen (upward swipe).

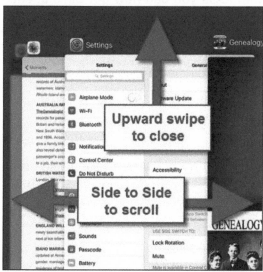

Android: You can press and hold the home button to find the apps you used most recently. However, Android doesn't struggle with multi-tasking apps using up resources the way iOS does. In fact tech advisors like AndroidTipsandHacks.com advise against constantly closing apps. That being said, if you ever want to see what's running in the background or close a particular app, it varies a bit from device to device, but usually it is triggered by a dedicated button. On my Samsung tablet it is a button to the left of the home button on the frame of the tablet. To close an app, just swipe it away.

Voice Command

Here are some secrets about Siri, and then I'll cover some alternatives on the Android side.

Siri

On an Apple device, Siri offers yet another way to navigate. By pressing and holding the Home button on your mobile, the familiar "What can I help you with?' request appears on the screen, and Siri is then ready to receive your verbal request (via your microphone). Here are some of my favorite ways to use Siri to my advantage while working on genealogy.

Go Hands-Free

Beginning with iOS8 you can now get Siri's attention and help without ever touching your iPhone or iPad. The "Hey Siri" feature uses your device's microphone to deliver your message.

How to enable Hey Siri:

1. Open your Settings

2. Tap General

3. Tap Siri

4. Slide the "Allow Hey Siri" slider so that it appears green.

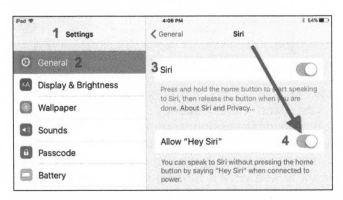

5. Follow the prompts for a few moments of quick Siri training. You will be asked to say "Hey Siri" and a few other phrases so that Siri can recognize and respond to your voice.

6. When you're done with the setup, head back to your home screen and give it a try. Simply say "Hey Siri." You will hear the familiar ding, the screen will go black, and "Hey Siri" will appear on the screen. Speak your command, and Siri will do the rest.

Wicked Wikipedia Search

Wikipedia has a wealth of information. When you're in the throes of your research, you can turn to Siri for quick and helpful information. For example, say to Siri "Wikipedia German History" and you'll instantly receive the relevant Wikipedia article outlining German history, complete with maps of changing boundaries and source citations.

Tap into Twitter

If you've ever attended a genealogy conference, then you are probably aware that there can be last minute classroom changes, special events and other news that occurs during the conference. Most major genealogy conferences (such as RootsTech, NGS, FGS) have Twitter accounts, and make announcements in real time on Twitter. Now you can ask Siri "what is RootsTech tweeting about?" and it will deliver the latest relevant tweets from the RootsTech Twitter account (@rootstech).

1. Press and hold down the Home button to activate Siri on your iPhone or iPad, or say "Hey Siri"

2. Say "What is RootsTech tweeting about?" Substitute *RootsTech* with the name of any Twitter account from which you want to receive updates.

3. Siri will then serve up the recent tweets by that specific Twitter account.

4. Tap on any tweet to read more, view details, or launch in the Twitter app.

How to Remember What You Can Ask Siri

Not sure what Siri can answer? Ask Siri "what can I ask you?" and you'll get a list!

Android Options

Covering voice command is trickier because there are different options depending on the device you have. S Voice is the voice assistant that ships with all new Galaxy devices, but it hasn't been met with rave reviews. My Samsung Tab A doesn't come with S Voice, so I will leave it to you to head to Google and run searches such as *What can I ask S Voice*. I'm going to offer up an alternative, and for those of you who like me don't have S Voice, it's a great solution. It's called Dragon Mobile.

How to get started with Dragon Mobile:

1. Download the free app

2. Confirm the name you want to be called

3. Select a Wake Up phrase (This helps Dragon respond to your voice only). The default is "Hey Dragon", but you can change that if you want.

4. Set up your Personal Options as desired.

You're ready to go!

I really like Driver mode, which lets me control my tablet "hands-free" and "eye-free" so I can pay attention to the road. You'll find it at Settings > In the Car > Driver Mode. You can manage when Driver Mode is initiated by tapping *Automatically Start Driver mode* and sliding the switch to *On*. From there you can turn on:

- while driving

- when placed in a car dock

- when a wired headset is plugged in

- when connected via Blue Tooth

Don't Enable Attentive Mode which allows you to wake up your device with Dragon even when the screen is off. If you enable it, your battery life will be negatively impacted. It will also prevent other apps, as well as your keyboard microphone, from recording audio. If you have trouble with your microphone, just go to Settings > MyAssistant > Attentive Mode and make sure it is disabled.

Functionality Tips and Tricks

Screen Shots

In order to clearly show you the various apps and techniques I've discussed in this book, I needed to capture images of my iPad's screen. I accomplished that by taking screen shots.

There are many other reasons you might want a picture of what appears on your device's screen. For example, when you want to review information found online during times that you won't have internet access. While I'm waiting to board a plane, I will often time just snap some shots of genealogy websites and blog articles so that I can read them in flight without paying for WiFi access.

iOS

Creating a screen shot with your iPad is easy to do. Simply press and hold the home button (the round button found at the bottom of the screen) and then quickly press the power button (at the opposite end of your iPad on the upper right metal edge) as if you were snapping a photo with a camera. In fact, if your iPad's volume is turned up you will actually hear the sound of a camera snapping a picture.

The image will be saved to your iPad's camera roll. From there you can tap the Share icon or save it to your Dropbox account.

Android

Screenshots can vary based on the type of Android device you are using. My Samsung tablet has a very cool way of taking screen shots. With the swipe of the side of my palm the task is done.

First, go to Settings to ensure that Palm Swipe to Capture is enabled. (Settings > Motions and Gestures > Palm Swipe to Capture.) Then, pull up anything you want on your screen, such as a birth record at FamilySearch.org. Turn your hand on its side so that the outer edge of your palm is touching the edge of the tablet's screen and swipe left to right or vice versa. I find it works best when the side of my hand from the tip of my pinkie finger to my wrist is doing the swiping. You'll hear the familiar camera-click sound and the screen will flash. This indicates that a photo of what appears on your screen is now in your Gallery.

Dictation

Tap the microphone on your keyboard (to the left of the spacebar) when you are creating an email, note, document, or searching the web, and speak what you want typed. You can even include punctuation. The dictation is usually quite accurate, even in somewhat noisy environments.

iOS

Enable Dictation in the Settings menu: Settings > General > Restrictions > Siri & Dictation. You will then see a small microphone icon appear on the lower left of your iPad's keyboard. However, be aware that you will need an Internet connection for the Voice Dictation feature to work.

If you have an older iPad (1 or 2) try downloading the free app Dragon Dictation (iOS).

Android

You should see a microphone on your keyboard, but again that depends on the device. On my Samsung the key next to the spacebar is a gear icon for Settings. Press and hold it and you will find the microphone. Tap it, and it will become the default for that key. From that key you can also access:

- clipboard
- handwriting pad
- keyboard styles including floating and split

Dragon Mobile Assistant by Nuance Communications is also an option. Learn more about it in the previous *Voice Command* section of this chapter.

Battery Boosts

You can always use more power, right? The good news is that there are steps you can take to maximize your device's power resources

iOS

Reduce the brightness of your screen in the Control Center we mentioned earlier or set it to Auto-Brightness in Settings.

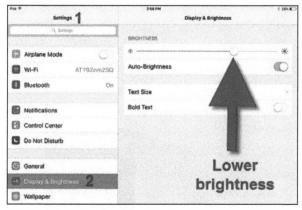

Turn off wireless items you are not using such as Bluetooth in your Settings

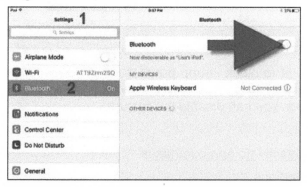

Limit the number of push-based notifications from your various apps (most apps ask you if you will allow pushed notifications)

Android

On an Android tablet you will also find Battery saving options. Power Saving mode performs several power-saving strategies simultaneously such as reducing the screen brightness, reducing frame rate, and limiting the maximum CPU performance. Or kick it into high gear with Ultra Power Saving Mode. This limits the number of usable apps, minimizes the Home screen layout, and turns off Bluetooth.

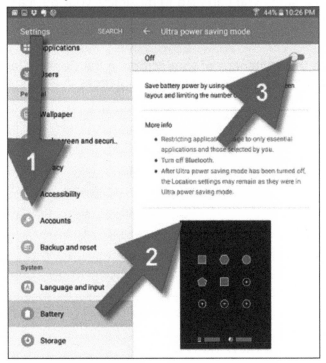

App Purchases Deactivation

If you want to block in-app purchases, or you want to prevent kids or grandkids that might use your iPad from making purchases, you can disable the feature.

iOS

How to deactivate app purchases:

1. Settings
2. General
3. Restrictions
4. Enable Restrictions

5. You will be prompted to enter a passcode

You can not only restrict in-app purchases by sliding the "In-App Purchases" to "Off," but you can also select the type of content that will be allowed.

Android

While you can't (currently) disable in-app purchases alone on Android, you can require that your Google account password must be entered before any purchase of any kind is made.

How to deactivate app purchases:

1. Open the Play Store
2. Tap the Menu icon (three horizontal lines) at the top of the screen
3. Tap Settings
4. Tap Require authentication for purchases.
5. Select For all app purchases through Google Play on this device
6. Enter your Google account password
7. Tap OK

App Related Tips and Tricks

Search Your Device

If you like to fill up your device with apps like I do, you will be glad the search screen is there. It is often quicker to do a search for an app than to swipe through various pages of apps and folders.

iOS

To access the search screen, swipe all the way to the right until the Spotlight screen appears. Or an even quicker way to get there is to swipe down from any Home screen. The Search box appears at the top.

Android

Swipe down from the top of the screen. Next tap the "S Finder" / magnifying glass icon to reveal the search box. Here you can search your device for apps, contacts, settings, email, files, messages and more.

Searching

Type a keyword or the name of the app that you are looking for in the search field. A list of apps matching the search words will instantly appear in the results list. Tap the app you want and you will instantly be taken to it.

The power of Search is not limited to apps. It can locate keywords in many of your apps like the Calendar, Contacts, Mail, Notes, Music, Reminders, Video, the Web, and more. While I hesitated using the search feature at first, it has proven itself time and again to be an incredibly efficient method for locating data, particularly on a heavily used tablet!

Deck the Dock

iOS only

You can add and rearrange the apps that appear in your dock (the bottom row of apps that remain stationary on your screen) by tapping and holding an app until they all start to "shake" and then dragging and dropping them to the desired location. You can have up to six of your most used apps in your dock.

Get Organized with Folders

Staying organized is important to genealogical success, and that applies to your tablet as well. You can create app folders with custom titles that go a long way to helping you keep your apps neat and tidy. The process is very similar between iOS and Android.

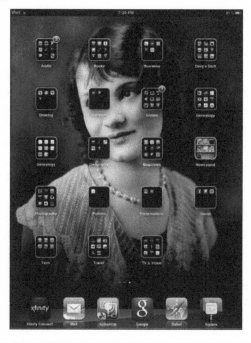

How to create a folder:

1. Press and hold any app (iOS: they'll start to shake)

2. Drag and drop one app on top of another which creates a folder.

3. Type a title for the folder in the field provided

4. Continue to drag and drop apps into the folder as desired

I like to create lots of folders and give them custom category titles. If you have many "pages" of apps on your tablet, you should seriously consider organizing them into categories for greater efficiency, and less swiping through multiple pages.

Folder Organization

You've now reduced the number of screens by combining similar apps and bookmarks into folders. But don't stop there! Now it's time to organize them in a way that will be meaningful and efficient for you. Here are ways to organize folders:

- *Use the chapter titles from this book as your guide.* I've already grouped apps by type for you which gives you a great place to start.

- *Alphabetize your folders.* Carefully and concisely name each folder and then move them around to be in alphabetical order

- *Place folders based on usage.* Are you right handed or left handed? Do you prefer to work at the top, center or bottom of the screen? Let your preferences guide you. Mentally rate your apps by the amount of usage and group them accordingly: Group 1 (I use these all the time), Group 2 (fairly regularly), and Group 3 (can't remember now why I downloaded these but I still want them around.)

Bonus Tip: If you're a visual person like me, it's quicker to interpret a picture than read the words. If that describes you, turn to Emojis! Apple and Android both feature Emojis in their native keyboards. All you have to do is press the folder and select the title to edit it. Press the space bar once after the title and then tap the Emoji symbol on the keyboard. Now you can pick from loads of pictures that represent the theme of the folder. When you find the right one, tap to add it and then close the folder. Now you can quickly visually scan your home screen for images rather than reading words. In fact, you can omit text titles all together if you locate the ideal emoji to convey the apps contained within.

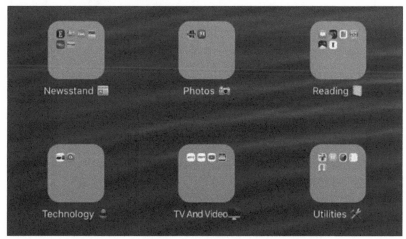

Android offers the added bonus of color coding your folders. Tap the folder and then tap the artist palette icon to select a color. I hope we see this on Apple products soon!

Create App-Looking Icons for Websites

While you wouldn't want an app for every single website that you use for genealogy, you probably have some serious favorites that you go to time and time again. Or perhaps you've found an intriguing site that you don't have enough time to devote to right now, but you want to keep it on your radar. Here's a really slick way to create an icon that looks like an app for your iPad's homepage. It will put you just one tap away from the best websites.

How to create an "App" bookmark:

1. Open the Safari (iOS) or Chrome (Android) app

2. Navigate to a website

3. Tap the Share button (iOS) or three stacked dots icon (Android) at the top of the browser

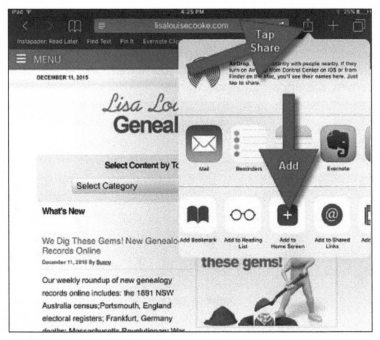

4. Select "Add to Home Screen" from the menu

5. Name your icon or use the name provided

6. Tap the "Add" button

7. An icon will be added to your home screen. *(Image below: iOS)*

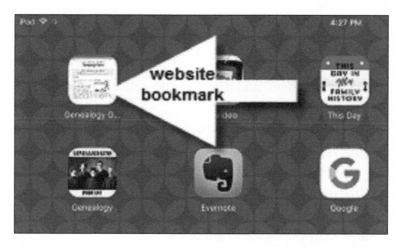

8. One tap of the bookmark icon will give you instant access to that website. *(Image below: Android)*

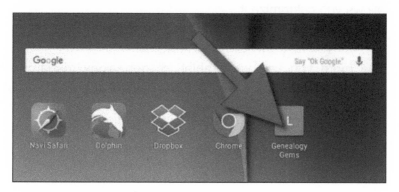

Why not create a folder of bookmarks of your favorite genealogy websites?

Organize What You Share

Over time you will certainly develop a preference for certain apps, and find yourself sharing to them again and again. Rearrange your share icons in the order of highest use and save yourself some time. I mentioned this briefly in the section on Evernote, but it's worth repeating in more depth here.

iOS

<u>How to rearrange your share icons:</u>

1) Tap the Safari app (or really any app that has a share feature)

2) Tap Share

3) Press, hold, and drag the app you use the most into first position on the left.

4) Continue dragging and dropping apps as desired

5) Tap More to see the full list of available apps, and activate any you think you may need in the future.

6) Tap Done

Android

<u>How to rearrange your share icons:</u>

To the best of my knowledge this little trick is only available on iOS. However, there is a nifty app called Andmade Share in the Play Store that replaces the system share menu and allows you customize it.

Undo / Redo

The more you use your tablet for genealogy research, the more typing you will likely do. The first time you need to erase an entire paragraph, you will find the backspace key a very impractical way to do it. Here are two solutions:

Undo Solution 1: Shake It Up

iOS

Yep, just like the Etch A Sketch of our childhood you can literally shake your iPad and up will pop a window offering you an "Undo Typing" button. A word of caution though, the iPad has a very slick back and a glass front. Not long ago I was sitting in a chair with my iPad on my lap and as I leaned over to reach for something the tablet turned into a flying saucer that flew off my lap and onto the tile floor. Yes, it has small cracks on one corner to prove it. I would think twice before shaking my iPad over a hard surface.

Android: Sorry, not available at the time of this writing.

Undo Solution 2: Undo Button

iOS

This is a more conservative approach to the Undo dilemma. You will find the Undo button on the numbers screen of the keyboard. This function actually requires two taps:

1. Tap the ".?123" button
2. Tap the "Undo" button

Android

At the time of this writing there is not an Undo button on the Android keyboard. However, the JotterPad – Writer app has one and it is free in the Play Store.

Redo

iOS

If you ever need to redo something you have just erased, you will find the "Redo" button is three taps away:

1. Tap the ".?123" button
2. Tap the "#+=" button
3. Tap the "Redo" button

Android

At the time of this writing there is not a Redo button on the Android keyboard. However, the JotterPad – Writer app has one and it is free in the Play Store.

Photo Slideshow

Every genealogist can use this next tip. Did you know that you can turn your tablet into a digital photo frame?

iOS

How to create a Slideshow:

1. Go to the Photos app
2. Select an album
3. Tap Slideshow in the top right corner
4. A slideshow will automatically begin

5. To customize, tap Options at the bottom left corner

6. Select the type of transition you want

7. Select the length of time each photo will display

8. Select the type of music you want, or none

Consider creating a number of albums in your Photos app library for various types of slide shows. Here's an example of the types of albums I have created:

- My family history photos

- My husband's family history photos

- Grandchildren photos

- Year in review photos

The combinations of music (that you can add to iTunes) and images (organized by topics into albums in your Camera Roll Library) are limitless!

Android

How to create a Slideshow:

1. Tap Camera

2. Tap your photos (small square in the right bottom corner of the screen)

3. Tap More

4. Tap Slideshow

5. Tap Slideshow Settings

6. You can select the type of transition effect you want and how long you want each photo to appear.

Part Four: Conclusion

Chapter 17: Mobile Genealogy Means Adventurous Genealogy

A Note from the Author: This chapter first appeared in Turn Your iPad into a Genealogy Powerhouse (2012). This book, as I've already mentioned, was born from that book. I thought about writing a new ending, but really, this story still perfectly conveys my feeling and thoughts about Mobile Genealogy:

Are you becoming a home computer potato? I liken this to the television couch potato. I won't disagree that it is pretty comfy on the sofa, or in front of our computer in our pajamas. But if your home computer is the only place you are conducting research on your family history, you are missing so much!

When I think of my Great Grandmother Louise Sporowski sewing her money into her petticoat and taking her four year old daughter by the hand to board a ship bound for America, I am awestruck. She made the journey essentially alone because her husband had already crossed the Atlantic to look for work. All this world traveling was happening before the airplane or high-speed rail was ever invented. (Oh, and did I mention that she was three months pregnant, and likely suffering from morning sickness as she faced the vast ocean?)

Louise was in search of freedom: freedom from toil in the hot, damp laundries (where she worked) and coal mines (where her husband worked) in Germany, freedom to own and work their own land, and freedom to educate her children as she saw fit.

After reading and working through this book, I hope you are feeling empowered to hit the road in the name of freedom:

Freedom from a view of your family history limited by the finite amount of documents digitized and online

Freedom from stagnation in your approach to research questions

Freedom to see your ancestor's world for yourself while still being "plugged in" and keeping your data updated and synchronized

When your tablet is equipped with the right apps, and you know the tips and tricks to squeezing the most out of it, then you are free to follow your ancestor's footsteps. I wish you safe travels and a lifetime of Adventurous Genealogy!

About the Author

Lisa Louise Cooke is the producer and host of *The Genealogy Gems Podcast*, and *Family History: Genealogy Made Easy* podcast. Both audio shows are featured in iTunes, and at www.genealogygems.com.

She is an international conference speaker, author, podcast producer (*Family Tree Magazine Podcast*) and author of several articles and videos for *Family Tree Magazine*.

A wife and mother of three grown daughters, and grandmother to two grandsons, she is devoted to helping families cultivate their place in history.